Hope for the Wounded Heart

Hope for the Wounded Heart

Healing Your Emotional Wounds Through Peaceful Living and Spiritual Grace

Deborah Kalinyak, M.S., L.M.H.C.

with L. Frances Coker

Day to Day Enterprises Oviedo, Florida

Cover Design by Jamon Walker
Mythic Design Studio
www.mythicstudio.com

Printed in the United States of America

05 04 03 02 01 10 9 8 7 6 5 4 3 2 1

First Printing: September 2001

Printed by QUESTprint

ISBN: 1-890905-14-3

Library of Congress Control Number: 2001093365

Published by

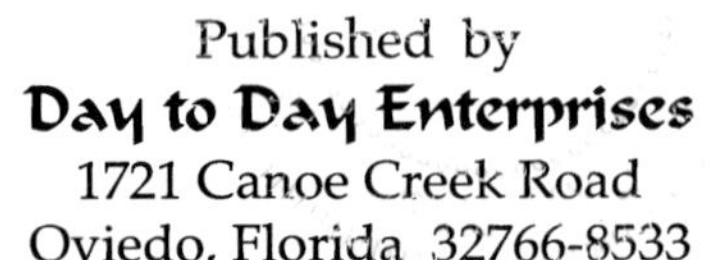
Day to Day Enterprises
1721 Canoe Creek Road
Oviedo, Florida 32766-8533
email: books@daytodayenterprises.com • (407) 359-9356
http// www.daytodayenterprises.com

Dedication

This book is especially dedicated to all those people who have been hurt in the name of religion, who grew up with a God who was portrayed to be mean. It also is dedicated to those people who, through the ages, have suffered physically and emotionally because some humans with religious authority thought they should.

My prayer is that you would come to know a loving and accepting God through the pages of this book which tells about my own journey in healing and spiritual grace.

Acknowledgements

First, I would like to gratefully thank God for helping me follow through on this book and for smoothing the way. Then I would like to thank my family, especially Andy, Krystle and Craig, and friends for their patience during the creative process and also for contributing prayers that appear in the book.

I would particularly like to thank L. Frances Coker, journalist, for her inspiration, patience and creative ability as we walked this road to publication together. For her continuing enthusiasm and encouragement, I thank Linda Humphrey, journalist and inspirational speaker. Then I also want to acknowledge the efforts and superb editorial advice of Carolyn Burns. Equally important to the success of this book are Christian evangelist, speaker and author Barbara Shlemon Ryan; Fr. Joseph Scerbo, S. A., Ph. D. and international president of the Association of Christian Therapists as well as the Rev. Robert Roach, school administrator, Presbyterian minister and former associate director and career counselor for JobLink. In particular I'd like to thank Mike Erdman for sponsoring this book.

Near and dear to my heart are my prayer partners in the Sacred Way Ministries and fellow members of the Association of Christian Therapists who were so supportive and encouraging during this process.

Finally, no acknowledgements would be complete without mentioning my dear parents. This book was written in memory of my parents Maureen and Dick who now are in their heavenly home with our Lord.

I thank you all for your prayers, thoughts and love,

Deborah Kalinyak.
Easter, April 15, 2001

With Hands

MyCinda Butterworth

With hands we serve.
With hands we pray.
With hands we soothe and comfort.
With hands we share and greet.
With hands we can nourish.
With hands we lift those who have fallen.
With hands we can do great things.
With hands we can reach out to others.
With hands we can caress and show affection.
With hands we can do many things.
Did not Christ's hands show how much he loves you?
Then how can we do less?

Preface

In the pages of this new book, the reader will find the journey of a unique soul who is stirred to bring the expression of herself onto the canvas of life, because of a new experience and understanding of God. In her opening chapter, entitled "The Good Catholic Girl," I was reminded of what psychologist Karen Horney said about "the tyranny of the should," and what holy men and women have taught us: that the Holy Spirit comes to disturb us and comfort the disturbed.

The author's journey will enable readers to look at their own distortions of the true and authentic images of God. The exercises at the end of each chapter are helpful. The experience of pain and emptiness, which the author begins to share with us, can become reminders that such experiences are often the fodder and the prod to new revelations of God's Peace beyond understanding. The journey toward healing is truly a descent, a downward movement beyond the fake promises and the lies we have accepted around our early root emotional pain. The step downward is paradoxically a step upward to new life in the Spirit. We move from denial toward awareness, from disowning toward response-ability and from withholding toward communication.

It was a joy for me to read of the "coming home" of the author to her unique gifts and talents. Deborah Kalinyak, and we, can live in the discovery of the truth the saints knew and proclaimed, "We are His Delight; no longer shall we be called 'forsaken.' "

I heartily recommend and urge those who hear the call to heal and be healed to find in this book that we, too, can allow the tender love of our God to penetrate our *will to life* and turn our stumbling blocks into stepping stones.

Fr. Joe Scerbo, S.A., Ph. D.
President, Association of Christian Therapists

Table of Contents

Foreword by Barbara Shlemon Ryan

Barbara Shlemon Ryan is president of Be-Loved Ministry and an internationally known speaker on spiritual healing. She is the author of five books on healing including **Healing Prayer** *and* **Healing the Hidden Self**. *She sits on the executive board of the world-renowned Christian Healing Ministry, founded by Francis and Judith MacNutt.*

"In my deepest wound I saw your glory and it dazzled me." St. Augustine.

It was a t-shirt that first drew us together. In the chapter of her book devoted to her call to the healing ministry, Deborah Kalinyak describes our first meeting in Gulf Shores, Alabama. We were both attending an international conference for the Association of Christian Therapists when she walked past me wearing a shirt with the name of a church my husband and I had recently joined. At the time of our brief conversation, neither Debbie nor I perceived a friendship blossoming which would produce great blessings for many others and us.

After returning to Florida we began meeting regularly to discuss our mutual desire to bring the message of healing to those who are in mental and emotional turmoil. Her lively personality and easy laugh initially brought a lift to my day. But I quickly learned that her hunger to touch hurting hearts was born from her own depth of sorrow.

In her book Debbie details her personal journey from the pit of despondency to the heights of joy. She candidly reveals an intimate portrait of her personal indiscretions, doubts and fears. Not content with merely narrating her own story, she has included mental health thoughts and prayerful meditations to guide the reader's quest for healing.

Debbie is fervent in her belief that everyone can achieve spiritual, emotional and physical renewal if they can break the chains that bind them to unhealthy styles of living. Many are stuck in mental patterns that keep them from living a victorious life. They are exhausted, burned out, unable to love themselves or others.

For several years I worked as a nurse in a government mental hospital. I would listen for hours as my patients described personal histories of life-long suffering and abuse. Often I would pray for enlightenment to bring freedom to these lost individuals.

God granted my request through a series of events that taught me the importance of healthy spirituality in order to attain soundness of mind and body. Nearly four decades of my own ministry have left no doubts. I know our destiny is to become 'fully human and fully alive.'

Debbie's book presents a guide to unlock the chains of doubt and fear so the real self may be revealed. Her writings are sure to strike a chord in the heart of all seekers of truth. Like me, I believe each will find her to be a friend who can be trusted carrying a message of healing and hope.

Barbara Shlemon Ryan,
Feb. 1, 2001

INTRODUCTION

For much of my life depression has been an ongoing and an unpleasant theme in my life. I've attempted suicide more than once. I've been a whiner. I've often seen myself as a victim and powerless. But now I'm free of that ugly past.

As co-author of this book I asked to write this introduction because I strongly believe in Deborah Kalinyak's concept of blending good spiritual health with good mental health. For me, the struggle to overcome depression and its attendant problems — lack of self-worth, dead-end careers, failed marriages and more — has been long and arduous. It wasn't until I began to put a spiritual element in my life that things began to come right.

I'm not sure you will believe me when I tell you this concept has validity without hearing my story, so I'm telling it. However, if you already agree with me about the connection between spiritual and mental health just skip ahead to chapter one. If you still need persuading, let me do that now.

Here's the rest of my story:

Even though I was in and out of depression and crises throughout my life, I always sought peace. But I almost always had just the opposite. Like a lot of people, either I was over the moon about some romance or drowning my sorrows in a pitcher of margaritas. I knew there had to be something more out there, I just couldn't quite put my finger on it.

I've had disastrous experiences with probably eight or nine psychologists — and a couple of psychiatrists — over more than 25 years of seeking help. I had tremendous help from two psychologists, but it took a new spiritual outlook to totally turn my life around.

About ten years ago I began to find answers, which soothed the craziness in my heart and soul. However, my life did not become perfect, nor do I ever expect it to be. Life and learning are an ongoing process: I'm still disorganized, I still have trouble balancing my checkbook. I still forget birthdays. I still have pride and humility issues. I still make promises I have a hard time keeping. The list goes on.

But today there is a big difference. Today there is peace and even joy in my life. I may have moments of real sorrow or even occasional pieces of anger, but I'm more content than I ever have been. The reason for this is that I've come to know that there is something so much bigger than me in this universe: namely, God. What I've learned is that I can give all my troubles to Him and because of that I can take my peace from Him.

Although He always was there for me, as He is for everybody, for years I denied it over and over again — preferring to party rather than hypocritically pray.

Meeting Debbie

It was during the time I was beginning to know God that I heard Deborah Kalinyak speak at a seminar. We met through mutual friends. Debbie, who is very friendly and easy to know, talked about God's compassion and love, not about an angry and vengeful God. I wanted to be able to trust something in my life and she taught me I could trust God. Her belief that mental health is influenced by spiritual health hit me squarely in the solar plexus because I had been out there seeking for a long time and always thought there had to be something more which could bring me the peace of mind I so desperately wanted.

It seemed like such a great concept that I asked Debbie after another one of her seminars why she hadn't written a book to help other people. (Journalists always see things as a possible story or book.) That was the beginning of our conversations that ultimately led to this book.

Since then I've been to Debbie's church and she's been to mine. Although she is a Catholic and I am a Protestant, we found we had many values in common, especially when it came to expressing God's love and mercy.

But let me get back to my story as it relates to the purpose of this book. As I see it, the purpose of this book is to help heal people of the pain; sorrow, anger, depression and disease brought on by the human condition. The book tells you about the author's pain and healing and it gives you mental health insights as well as spiritual ones. One can live, just live ... or one can experience joy, contentment and peace. I finally chose the latter, but first I had to go through my own hell.

Life Before

Growing up I went to Sunday school by myself — dropped off and picked up — but wasn't taught much about God or living a spiritual life until I was 9-years-old. I had just turned 9 the week before I was unceremoniously dropped into a Protestant boarding school where I would live until I graduated, just before my 18th birthday. (Yes, I did go home for summer and holidays.)

At that school we went to chapel twice a day. While there was talk of God, it pretty much all went over my head. I was so miserable about being deserted by my family (or so I thought) that I missed just about all the God-stuff, especially about His love and mercy for me. I felt lonely, unwanted and unworthy of love.

My parents had divorced when I was a baby and when I met my father for the first time shortly after I graduated from the boarding school; he asked me a very pointed question. "Are you saved?"

I said no.

I wasn't really sure what that meant. Back then, it seemed to me, we didn't talk much about being saved. But being a smarty-pants, about-to-be college freshman I said I was probably agnostic. (A good exercise in psuedo-intellectuality.) My father's disappointment in the face of my need to be loved set me on a twenty-year search for a God with whom I could live. Very ironic. I was looking for a God who would love me no matter what and He was there all along, loving me. I just wouldn't acknowledge Him because somehow I thought He disapproved of me, like I thought my father did.

Before I write another word I must tell you that I now see how much my father loved me, even then. He had this special thing which he wanted to share but all my immature ears could hear was his seeming disapproval which I then turned into God's disapproval. Being my father's daughter I was pretty stubborn. Even stubborn about coming to God.

The years that ensued led to two divorces, heavy drinking and a lot of looking for love in all the wrong places. I threw myself into the new age movement, even working for a while as a psychic, which was pretty stupid. How could I help other people with foreknowledge when I, myself, was so messed up? Even then, I believe, God was calling because He always seemed to give me words of comfort and suggestions for a spiritual, churchly life for the people I spoke to. There now, *all* my dirty laundry is hung out (but has since been cleaned, if you get my drift).

When my daughter became a teenager, we began going to church "for her." I was very afraid of what the "church" had in store for me. Would they tell me I had it all wrong? Would they reject me? Would they disapprove? In some cases they did. That was hard, really hard. But I got fed enough that after awhile I stopped fighting. To those who fed me God's love: I am so grateful.

Life After

My life began to change, bit by bit, for the better. I became extremely sorry for all the crazy stunts I had pulled, for all the major sins I had committed. I haven't murdered anybody or stolen anything, but I've pretty much wallowed in the mud I created of the other eight commandments. I had hurt a lot of people and it was not a pretty picture at all. I wanted to be forgiven.

I had heard about the idea of redemption before, but Debbie was the first person I actually listened to. She was the first person who suggested I delve deeper into the spiritual life which God offered (or at least she was the first who got through to me).

Debbie had a peace about her that I wanted so I was open to her message. And whenever I heard what she had to say about God, it made sense, so I came to believe I could trust it. Besides, her peacefulness spoke volumes for the truth of her message.

At the same time we began talking about doing a book together our friendship was growing. One day, rather boldly I told her she was lucky because I had stuff that always would haunt me and she wasn't carrying that kind of baggage. I assumed that the reason she was so peaceful was because she hadn't had to deal with the same sort of horrible stuff I had.

She Gets My Undivided Attention

Right then and there she began to tell me her story. It was pretty compelling. How does one emotionally heal from the murder of a loved one? Debbie's emotional and spiritual health came courtesy of God's love and mercy, after she prayed for help. (Read the book, it's all in there.)

We Contemplate a Book...

It seemed to me she had a very important message that would help other people and her personal story would make the book even more compelling—*especially* since she's a mental health counselor. So I told her she should share her story when writing her book.

We talked some more about the book, but both of us had busy lives and it never seemed to be the right time. Two years went by. Meanwhile, I was being healed spiritually more and more. I was coming to my own peace.

When I moved my office I began to get these urges that the time was right to do the book. I faxed Debbie a suggested schedule. She also had been getting little pushes to do the book. We prayed about it and came to realize that it was God's book, meant to heal people of their emotional pain. You'll read more about this in one of the chapters.

With No Preaching, No Condemning

As we began to work together, getting Debbie's story and mental health thoughts down, I would think of one person or another who I knew could be helped by a particular section or chapter. I'd think, "I wish Susie or Sammie or Zack (not real names) could hear this right now." I kept telling Debbie how many people I thought it would be helping once we finished. Even though several years before we had talked about doing a book, seeing those words in black and white and knowing they actually could help someone inspired us to keep going.

But many of us, myself included, have had a struggle with people from various religions who seem to put obstacles between us and the joy and peace God has to offer. I'm sure since the book is broad in its approach and does not take into account the various precepts, dogmas and doctrines of individual denominations that there will be some who think we have said too much and others who will think we didn't go far enough. But, to me, this book simply is about being healed by God's peace and grace. It does not preach, nor does it condemn. It does offer help and a way to find out for yourself all about the love, joy and peace which God offers.

Simplicity Itself

We've tried to keep the book simple so that those in most distress might be spoon-fed God's grace. When I was young, living on my grandfather's cattle farm in Maryland, I had an aunt who would rescue baby birds that had fallen out of the nest and otherwise might die if not for her tender care. She would take these defenseless, featherless birds and hand feed them with an eyedropper until they thrived and learned to fly.

That's what I personally hope this book will do for you.

L. Frances Coker
Sept. 8, 2000

Dear Heavenly Father,
Who knows what it is that makes us turn from ourselves
and toward you and then desire to come even closer to you?
Maybe it's in the depths of our darkest tragedies
or the heights of our greatest joys and triumphs.
Whatever it is, help us recognize You in it when it occurs
and to then see you and further seek you
in the ordinariness of our everyday lives.
Amen

All my love, Andy
(Andrew Kalinyak)

Chapter 1

The Good Catholic Girl

Under the altar at Our Lady of the Lakes Catholic Church, I was a mess. As I lay in the fetal position, I could smell leftover incense and faded flowers.

The church was spookily empty.

But the fact that the church's double front doors had been left open at night, even though no one was there was one of those weird coincidences.

I had been crying off and on for months. My best friend was dead and I wanted to be. I was under the altar because it was the only safe haven I knew. I was toe to toe with death and not sure if I wanted to leave this planet or stay.

Either way, I was sure I was going to be miserable. I was desperate for relief from a devastating heaviness that had dogged my every step for six months.

Her name was Patricia. She had been my best friend, but in 1979 she had been kidnapped, strangled and then shot execution-style in the head. The killer had shot her boyfriend sixteen times. Then the killer had put the two of them into a camper and left them at a Florida highway rest-stop.

Their decomposing bodies were found ten days later. Her body was so gone that the only way of identifying her was through dental records.

The murder has never been solved.

I couldn't conceive a 21-year-old woman being dead. I thought about and literally felt her physical pain. She had been such a kind, caring person, always someone that I could count on. We met at my first job and had known each other for four years.

After her murder I'd wake up in the middle of the night in total sweats and pain throughout my body. I didn't want to believe I had been instrumental in getting her together with the guy who had gotten her killed. But I had.

Overwhelming Guilt

My guilt was overwhelming. I had helped her get together with him (the boyfriend with whom she was killed) because of an abusive relationship she had with another boyfriend. That first boyfriend had been not only physically abusive but controlled every move she made. She couldn't go anywhere without calling *him* and letting *him* know where she'd be and what she'd be doing — even though she was old enough to be living in her own apartment and on her own. *He* would let no one near her and hardly even let her go to her mother's house.

When she started to talk about someone else she'd met in the hospital — she had just gotten her nursing license — I encouraged her to seek out this new guy. He was training to be a physical therapist.

The first day I heard about the new guy, I was at her apartment and she had a big smile on her face.

She said, "I met this guy in the hospital. He's so cute. He wants me to come over today, but I'm scared to go because *you-know-who* might find out."

"I'm here," I said to her. "Why don't we go together? Do you know where this guy lives?"

"He's only a few blocks away," Pat said.

So we took off in my ancient 1966 Mustang and when we got there, he met her at the door. I can still see the scene clearly today, more than twenty years later. He invited us in. I stayed just long enough for them to get comfortable with each other and then I left. They fell in love that day.

She had a hard time getting rid of the old boyfriend. She

never told me but I knew he beat her up at least one more time because I saw bruises all over her arms, neck and face.

For Pat, perhaps it was a case of that expression about trading one bad situation for another — "out of the frying pan and into the fire" — because the new boyfriend didn't seem like a prize catch either.

After I got to know this new boyfriend, I noticed he was very sarcastic and a wiseguy ... always had an answer for everything. Like most people our age, Pat and I had smoked an occasional joint together. I was only 18 years old and still scared to death of my father, that's what kept me from being a pothead. But, after meeting this new boyfriend, she started to smoke pot heavily every day and to experiment with other recreational drugs that he introduced her to.

And the new boyfriend had lots of drug connections.

I started to back away from Pat and all of that because it was more than I wanted to get into. I also had met a new friend in college who I wanted to hang out with and get to know better.

One day Pat called me and said she and the new boyfriend had purchased a house out in the middle of an orange grove north of Orlando. She said no one could find their way in unless they were shown — which fit because there were people Pat and I knew together who would tell me that her new boyfriend was getting to be a big-time drug dealer for that area.

The thing about that house in the middle of the orange grove — it was the perfect hideout for all his deals, paraphernalia and even a few marijuana plants.

Poor Pat, she was so naive. She was just in love. Her parents were much older, in their late sixties or early seventies, when she was a teenager. She had been a change-of-life baby. She had no relationship with her father at all and her mother was pretty cold, so she was hungry for love. That's what was important to her, that someone love her, even if the love wasn't very good for her. She allowed all this because she wanted to be loved.

I kept telling her I had this prickly, terrible intuition that something was wrong every time I came out to the house in the orange grove. I didn't like going there at all. When he would come home, I'd leave.

He'd laugh at that, saying, "You think I'm evil or something."

And I really did think he was evil, so he was right.

Most of the time Pat and I would meet somewhere like the mall because I hated going over to the house in the orange grove. I just couldn't stand being near him or even in the same place with him.

He was obnoxious as hell, but worse still, it seemed like he had no soul. There was an evil emptiness to his eyes that really bothered me. They were like glittering metal that you couldn't see into.

I drifted further away from Pat because I was afraid of being arrested with her and her boyfriend. I knew the word was out about him and his dealings.

I really tried to warn her but, to this day, I wonder if I couldn't have done more.

However, I also knew if I was with them when they got in trouble, I'd be in trouble too. I thought of that a lot when I was around them and it made me afraid for them and for myself.

Right before Christmas that year, Pat invited me over to exchange Christmas gifts. She gave me a backgammon board, which I still have today. I didn't know how to play. He wasn't there because she knew I wouldn't come or stay if he was there. So she proceeded to teach me how to play backgammon and then she beat the heck out of me for 12 games. I won the 13th. He showed up on the 14th and I left.

We had laughed and had a really good time. As I was leaving, I told her I'd call her.

That was the last time I would see her alive. Less than a month later she was dead.

My First Spiritual Crisis

At that time I was working for the Telephone Company in the accounting department. One day I received a call from my father.

He just said, "Come home."

That was the family code for something was terribly wrong.

As I drove home everything I could think that could possibly be wrong was going through my mind. When I entered the block I lived on, I saw my other close friend's car parked in our driveway. Then I knew something was wrong if she was there. As I got out of my car, I was shaking. My mother and father met me at the door.

They told me to come in and sit on the couch; they had something to tell me. They proceeded to tell me Pat had been killed and how: that she and her boyfriend had been found together, shot.

I started to cry. My mother, a nurse, knowing how painful the news would be, was ready with the Valium. My friend sat next to me on the couch comforting me.

The next few days were a blur, but I remember during the wake that Pat's picture was on top of a closed casket because she was so decomposed.

Despite the blur I remember vividly part of the funeral. It was a Catholic Mass and all her druggie friends were there. I sat with her mother and father and brother.

Her mother turned to me and asked, "How could this happen?"

I had no answer. I was numb and angry at the same time.

Her father kept saying, "I want to see her, I don't believe it's her."

Her brother had been in a motorcycle accident five years earlier and was brain-damaged, so he sat in silence. I'm not even sure he understood. Pat always said she'd take care of him after her parents died.

I wondered who would take care of him now.

After the service, we drove to the graveside. The priest said a few prayers. I remember walking away from there, thinking, "She was so young. God, how could you take her, she was only 21."

I was so mad then; just angry with the whole world — and God.

Back at work I had no ability to concentrate. I cried all the time and made terrible errors in my work. My boss usually was very hard-nosed but because this was all over the papers and television, she felt sorry for me. She gave me printouts to put in books and that's all I was capable of doing.

I progressively got more and more depressed.

I thought it was my fault Pat had died.

I stopped eating.

I only had enough energy to get up, go to work and come home and go to bed.

This went on for months, until it reached a crisis as surely as a life-threatening infection will come to a crisis in the body.

One night, I came home and I had so little energy I had to use my hands to lift my legs out of the car. I used the car door to pull myself out of the car. I knew I was in trouble. I went in and went to bed.

But the next day in desperation, instead of going home, I went straight to my church after work.

I pulled into the parking lot. I was frantic to get rid of my horrible, overwhelming depression. I wanted someone, anyone, to talk to about this. I needed relief from the guilt, pain and suffering. I went to the front door of the church because I didn't know where to go, how to get in or how to find someone like a priest. I figured the main door would be locked but, to my surprise, it wasn't.

So I went in. I looked all around for someone to help me.

When it became apparent that there was no one there for me, I had an urge to run and get under the altar. What else could I do? I lay there and cried out loud to God, "If you are really God and really here, please, please help me. I can't take it anymore."

That Was the Beginning of an Unusual Journey Toward Mental and Spiritual Healing

Finally, I stopped crying but, still sniffling, I crawled out from under the altar and headed toward the big double doors at the entrance to the church. My head was still hanging and my nose was still running. I was still miserable. But just as I touched the double doors and started to open them I had my first experience of God's supernatural power. It was as real and tangible as my car, desk or kitchen sink are real in my life now.

For months I had been physically hunched over, feeling like I had been carrying a ton of cement blocks on my back. Walking away from the altar those blocks were still there but when I touched the double front doors leading to the outside, something miraculous happened. I felt the weight literally being lifted off my back. As heavy as that load had been, it no longer was there. He had answered my cry for help and for the first time in six months I could stand up straight.

Help had arrived

I was exhausted and went to bed early that night, around nine. I slept better than I had in months. I had a dream that my friend Pat came to my bedroom.

"I've been hurting for you and feeling your pain," I told her.

"Are you alright?" I asked in a sort of one-sided conversation.

Then she answered me.

"I am alright," Pat said. "But you've been holding me back with your grief. I can't go on while you feel so much grief. I want you to let go of me, so I can go on."

I didn't know what that meant but she seemed to know. I felt a great peace come over me.

"I'll let you go and move on," I said, because I could see the desire in her eyes to move on.

That was a turning point for me. After the dream things really were better and I began to live again. About a month later I met my future husband.

What God had Meant to me Before my Extraordinary Experience

It seemed to me that God had first spoken to me in that church. I wasn't sure what it all meant. I wasn't particularly religious. My mother made only brief mentions of God's power as I was growing up.

Even though she talked about God working on our behalf, helping us, you couldn't tell by her behavior that she believed it. She didn't seem to see that He was working, because she never stopped worrying. In other words, she knew how to pray but, because she didn't know how to give her problems to God, she never had the peace that I wish she could have had.

I wished later she could have had the kind of peace that

I felt the day I crawled under the altar, cried to God, and walked out of the church released from the bondage of six months of overwhelming grief.

Growing up, there rarely was mention of God, or even prayer. Yet, my mother still seemed to be a person who had that connection with God. Because she was a nurse, she always was a caretaker. She was the one who made us all go to church and I mean MADE us go. What normally happened on Sunday morning, was that my brother and I whined, and I mean *whined*, about going and we argued.

"You can give one hour to God a week — get dressed," was the standard reply in my house when we complained and whined about going to church. Then, most of the time we didn't even talk to each other all the way there. I remember sitting in the pew with my mother and she would sing so loud that all three of us — my brother, my dad and I — would move away to not be embarrassed.

When I was little everything was in Latin and I never understood anything anyway. My mother bought my brother and me these little prayer books in English so we could follow the mass.

Then, when I was around age 6, my brother and I had to go to CCD, the Baltimore Catechism religious classes.

And, my brother and I whined even louder.

"Well you have to make communion so you have to go to the classes," my mother would say.

The strangest thing about first communion was the whole cultural thing that surrounded it. I remember it not being so centered on God as it was dressing up and looking like a bride. And when I received the bread for the first time, I remember squirming because it tasted like cardboard.

But I was beautiful — my mother told me so — and I did get a lot of presents.

Still, my mother was a great role model, sharing her faith through her example. She would go out of her way for people. She made us go through our closets and give to the poor. She'd invite strangers to Thanksgiving dinner who had no other place to go. She lived that Servant life. And if you took her coat she'd give you her shirt. That's the way she was. When something went wrong in our house, my mother would make the standard cup of tea, which was her way of offering comfort.

She'd do those things but never tell us to pray or tell us how God could help. God was very separate from our life. We lived here and He was up in heaven somewhere supposedly watching over us.

We would visit Him once a week.

The biggest thing mentioned was the Rosary. If there were a major, major crisis she'd give me a Rosary and tell me to pray the Hail Marys and the Father until it was finished.

"It's very powerful, " my mother would say, "my grandmother prayed it everyday."

No more explanation than that.

My father seemed even less interested in God-related matters. He was into worldly things, like a true salesman. When we were growing up, very often there was panic, terror, worry, anxiety, tension and stress surrounding the family financial situation. We never knew whether we would have a house to live in, food on our table and clothes on our backs. I grew up learning to be fearful, even outright scared, because I might not have a place to sleep or a house to live in.

My father tried to reassure us, "As long as we have each other, we'll be okay," he would say.

But the concept of God was so far from our household that I wouldn't think of Him or that He could help us in anyway. We didn't even have a Bible. My mother used to say, "Only the priest can interpret the Bible and read it to us. That's what we go to church for."

When I was confirmed at the age of 12, again I had no idea what that all meant, except it meant the end of CCD classes.

"Thank God," I thought at the time because I hated those classes. They were the most boring classes to sit through. There definitely was nothing inviting about this God-thing in those classes.

The closest I got to God at that time was watching my mother's unconditional love for people. When I would ask her how she could give unconditional love like that, she'd say, "It's because I have a lot of faith in God."

People surely loved her. You could just see it, but I hadn't achieved her faith yet.

That was my childhood introduction to God.

But after my supernatural-God experience I was never the same. You'd think that would have made things easy for me to open up to God. But it didn't. Instead of having the feeling that I could access God's power, I started to have more of a conflict with it.

Mental Health and Spiritual Thoughts

The way I felt during that time of mourning was just the same as what I imagine most of my clients feel when they first walk through my door. I had begun to realize I didn't want to live the life I was living at the moment. I wanted something better, more peaceful, more loving — definitely more spiritual. I wanted answers.

Just as I was searching for answers then, I know my clients also are looking for answers.

They probably have exhausted every possible solution and situation they could think of while looking for their problems to be fixed.

Now, in desperation, they are reaching out. They think they are totally alone. They think they're the only ones in the universe who have had this experience — whatever the experience is.

They have found themselves taking a plunge into an area they know nothing about and often feel like a failure because they haven't been able to fix this thing themselves.

They've tried — maybe more than once — to make their lives come right; only to have things crumble around them all over again. They don't know how to break the cycle of darkness and they may have that same stuff or problems start all over again. It's such a hopeless and helpless feeling. I know I felt like I was in a deep pit looking up and I'm sure my clients feel the same way when they first arrive. It feels like their only hope is the light at the top of the pit and sometimes that's pretty dim.

But there they are, walking through my doorway. They've taken one more step and that's important. They are desperate for change and they have at least a tiny glimmer of hope that things can change. I believe in hope. Hope is what keeps you going.

Exercise

When you've experienced emotional pain you need help to get through the distress. Counseling or talking it out with a trusted friend will help in the letting go process. Sometimes, however, people haven't even gotten to point where they can talk about it.

It's so important not to hang on to emotional pain. It robs you of your energy and takes a heavy toll on your body. You can end up feeling exhausted physically and emotionally. That's why it's important to begin the process of letting go. One of my favorite exercises to help people move through the process and begin to find peace is the following:

Get a plain piece of paper and a pen. On the top of the page write, "Dear God." Now tell God how you feel about the pain in your life. God has big shoulders, so just let it rip. Don't hold back. Put it all down. Then sign it with your name.

That felt good, didn't it? Now, you may think you are finished but this is only the first part of the exercise.

Turn the paper over. At the top write "Dear (your name)," and have God write a letter back to you. Remember we have a loving God who only wants the best for you. Close your eyes and sit a moment in silence. Feel the love of your Creator. When you're ready, open your eyes and let Him gently guide you through the response. Listen to your heart. Then sign the letter, "Love, God." (If you are too angry to write the response from God now, give yourself some time, remember you are human. Continue reading this book and maybe later you'll want to come back to this exercise. It's here for you if you ever want to do it.)

Prayer

Dear God,

When we're in the middle of despair help us to feel your love, to find you in the darkness. We need to know that we're not alone, that you are gently guiding us through our pain. Allow us to see the hope, which your love offers. Teach us and help us to be patient and to hang on when we can't see our way out of the desert of despair. Guide our every moment until we see the light. *Amen.*

God,
You know where I walk
and it's not always
upon the path of you.

You know the conflicts within me
and the choices I make
with such a limited view.

For no matter how far away
when I can no longer reach
that's when You take my hand.

And that's when I become open
to all Your possibilities
and to Your glorious plan.

Open me to You, Lord.

Love, Lola
(Lola Giacona)

Chapter 2

The Conflict Within

Although it was 1980, I was a still a child of the 1970s, what can I say? Now, looking back, I am embarrassed, even mortified that I acted the way I did but like so many of us I was a product of our time. "Sex, drugs and rock 'n' roll" ruled our universe, even when we knew better. I was pretty much like your ordinary 20-year-old trying to find my way in life, trying to fit in with my peers.

Deep within me, it seemed like two different people were living: One, who loved to party, drink, dance and fit in; the other one knew there was a God watching over me who had healed my life in sheer moments.

I was torn. Totally torn.

I was still hanging out in bars on Saturday night dragging myself home at four in the morning, only to get up at ten to make it to church.

When I got to church I would always have so much guilt and shame. The shame would wash over me and it would be almost paralyzing. I thought about not going to church anymore so I wouldn't have to feel the shame and guilt.

But then again I wanted to be there because I felt like I owed God my life.

Still, I wasn't ready to make the commitment to change my life, to change my "wicked, wicked ways." I was having way too much fun and just didn't want to stop, not even for the God who had lifted that terrible two-ton-cinder block nightmare of sadness off my shoulders.

During the time just before Pat's death, I had begun hanging out with another girlfriend named Theresa (not her real name), because Pat had become nearly inaccessible now that she had a new boyfriend. Theresa would go out to the bars with me and we'd get wasted. We'd go out two or three nights a week. We were both in community college and we both had full-time jobs but that didn't stop us. We were enjoying our first real taste of the world and our independence.

As I said, we'd go out and party on Saturday night, then the next day we'd go to church together. We'd talk about all the stuff we did the night before on the way to church but even that didn't stop us from going out again on the next Saturday night.

But church must have been having some effect because I began to realize that the time for me to settle down and get married might be approaching.

Within months of that realization, I met Andy, my future husband. Things were getting serious and we were engaged on my 21st birthday in November. We married in July the following year while I was still only 21.

Theresa was in my wedding.

On a Friday night in early August, not even a month after Andy and I were married, Theresa was in a terrible car accident. Her date was killed. She was pried out of the car with the jaws of life and taken to the hospital where she was put into intensive care.

Theresa didn't have family in Florida. After the police finally located her family, her brother had called a friend of mine who called me. By the time I heard about her being in the accident it was nearly 24 hours later on a Saturday night. I went to the hospital right away because I knew she was all alone. Meanwhile, her family who lived in the Mid-West was on its way.

When I walked into the hospital I told the nurse I was Theresa's sister in order to get in to see her.

"She's very sick and very critical," the nurse said before she let me into the intensive care unit. "We don't know if she'll make it. Her brain is swollen and we're removing fluid, if she does live, we don't know if she'll have brain damage or not."

As I entered I realized the nurse had been right. Theresa *was* a mess. You certainly couldn't recognize her under all the bandages and there were tubes everywhere. I stood there hurting for her and feeling like there was nothing I could do. And there wasn't much point in hanging around because she was in a coma.

I had to admit to myself that I *did* know what I could do for Theresa, I could pray for her. But I thought to myself, "Oh my God. How is my God going to hear me now after I have not listened to Him for one second, not heard Him, not changed my life in any way."

Yet, I felt like God was the only one I could go to in any of this.

It was my second wake-up call.

I remember saying to him, "I lost one best friend God, I can't lose another one."

After I left her in the intensive care unit, I asked Andy to drive me to the closest Catholic Church. We got there just before they were going to proceed down the aisle at the beginning of Saturday night mass. I had just a moment to ask the priest to pray for her and go see her in the hospital after mass. Then I lit a candle for her and we sat down for the service.

During the mass, the priest got up and said there was a young girl who had been in a terrible car accident and she was hanging on to life by a thread. He asked the congregation to pray for her. Then everyone said, "Lord, hear our prayer, that she will be healed."

I already knew there was power in prayer because I had been healed. I could only hope that it would work this time because I couldn't go through it all again.

The Miracle of Recovery

Theresa was in intensive care for about a month. While she was recovering she became child-like because of the brain injury. She didn't know who I was or anyone else. She had problems with memory. They couldn't tell if she was going to remain in that state or recover.

She returned home with her family after three months in the hospital. Once back in the Mid-West, Theresa began to piece her life back together. As the swelling went down she started to remember more and more. A year passed and she returned to Florida.

Her recovery was a true miracle. The only thing that still affected her was her sense of balance. Ultimately, though, even that got a bit better.

A year later she re-kindled an old romance and got married.

Getting Closer all the Time

I never went back to that priest, but I was sure his prayers and the prayers of that congregation had made a difference in Theresa's survival and recovery.

Knowing this brought me back to my crossroads. God had been good to me once again.

Was I expected to do anything in return?

I sort of wanted to do *something* in return. My gratitude was boundless. How could I maintain that feeling of gratitude and still live my former life?

It was like living a lie.

It definitely was living in conflict.

I felt like God expected me to make a decision in my life.

It was getting harder and harder to live in two worlds. I surely didn't want to go through any more big wake up calls. I'd had enough.

I pondered about leaving my old life and becoming a "Jesus-freak," as they used to call them and I definitely didn't want to be labeled as a Jesus-freak. I didn't want to be different, I just wanted to fit in with everyone else.

Thoughts are There, but the Will is Not

Clearly, at this time, the idea of ending this conflict was there but I still was struggling with giving up what I thought I'd have to give up. I thought my friends would go away and my family would disown me and think I was crazy.

But I began to be more and more thirsty for knowledge of this strange and powerful God who could do supernatural things just by my asking for them.

At this time I was still working for the Phone Company. There were two women in the accounting department with me. They were good pray-ers.

They both were Protestant, which is significant.

I came to learn that when you pray God hears you, no matter what religion you are.

Both of these women were very gentle and sweet. Whenever I was struggling with something they'd say, "we'll pray for you."

When they told me that, I knew I could trust what they were saying: I knew they *would* pray. Their very presence and belief in God's love comforted me. I knew their prayers for me would be heard. I just knew it.

Other People's Prayers

One day at break time, they invited me to go downstairs with them to pray in a circle with them. They prayed the most beautiful prayers out loud. And they didn't care what anyone thought of them. I felt like God was gently nudging me in the direction towards Him and His ways.

I just held hands with them. I let them pray because they knew how. I'd never been taught to pray out loud or to just talk to God like they did. Before this, I always used God in crisis only. But to tell him about every little thing, I didn't consider that to be an option. I only bothered Him with the big stuff. These two women, Barbara and Sylvia, taught me I could talk to God about everything, like I talked to my closest friends.

Before I knew it, I was developing a relationship with this God who had been so far away yet had answered my prayers. I was starting to make a real commitment to God.

Pretty soon we had a Bible study going on at lunch on Wednesdays. Of course, it was ecumenical, there were all kinds of faiths in that room. I learned that there were a lot of great people involved with getting to know God.

And, I didn't consider any of them Jesus-freaks.

I was growing in my faith. And, although I was still a bit apprehensive, I felt comfortable with these people. They were very loving and encouraging. I looked forward to seeing them every Wednesday. I trusted them and they stood by me. When things were difficult in my life, they prayed for me and things would get better or they wouldn't feel as bad as they had before.

They were teaching me about God's love.

I already knew about the love of God, after all, hadn't He performed two miracles in my life?

My prayer partners would tell me about having quiet time with God and how they'd read scripture everyday. One particular older woman completely inspired me. She was so peaceful and calm, yet she, like many of us, had so many crises in her life. Her faith was inspiring.

Because our Bible study could only meet once a week together, the people in the group encouraged me to get involved in my local church.

So Andy and I started going to a Re-New group during Lent, which is the church season just before Easter. Lent is a remembrance of Christ's temptation in the desert and a preparation for Easter.

Andy and I were the youngest in the group by 40 years. We studied the Sunday readings the week before they were read in church. I got to ask all kinds of questions that were bubbling up inside me.

Conflict Again

After Easter when the Re-New group stopped meeting, however; our thoughts began to turn more to home and family. Andy and I decided it was time for me to get pregnant. We had been married for three years. By fall I was pregnant and we were so happy. But on Christmas Day I miscarried. It was a very sad time for both of us.

I became angry with God. After all, *I felt I had done my part.*

I was making an effort to learn all about Him. I didn't understand how even though I had made this connection with God there still could be suffering in my life.

I sort of had this dreamy thought that if I knew God, nothing would go wrong in my life. I wouldn't have to suffer because He would take care of everything. I thought I would be protected and shielded from suffering by Him.

That's what I thought then and that was the beginning of my crisis in faith.

Mental Health and Spiritual Thoughts

When my clients come to me and begin counseling they often say after a few sessions, "I did everything I was supposed to do.

How come I'm not better yet?"

They, too, have a crisis in faith. As a counselor, I represent their hope to get better. The crisis arises when they don't achieve instant results. They think that because they've taken the first step, everything should automatically fall into place. But the truth is, it's only the first step. They've taken 20 to 30 years or more getting into this mess and it's going to take them a while to get out of it.

That's where commitment comes in. Just as God asks for a commitment in faith, counseling also requires a commitment toward mental health and a balanced life style. To me, making a commitment to both God and a balanced life style increases your chances of finding good mental health.

Why a balanced lifestyle? Because good mental health, I believe, rests on balance. I tell my clients it's like a four-legged table.

One leg, which represents your mental health, won't support the table unless the other three also do. That mental health leg includes your thoughts. How well are your thoughts? Are they positive or negative (The answer to that lies in the counseling.)

The second leg is emotional health. The question to ask is, how are your feelings? Do they match your thoughts? Do you live in joy or despair? (This too is addressed in counseling).

The third leg is physical health. Ask yourself: Am I eating right? Getting enough sleep and exercise?

The fourth and, to me, the most important leg is your spiritual well being. Ask yourself: Do I connect to the Higher Purpose in my life. Am I living an honest life before God? I always say to myself and to my clients when I know them better: Are you living your honest truth — not your likeable or made-up truth for your friends and acquaintances, but the genuine truth before God?

As they say, the truth will set you free.

Once you have the four legs of the table in place you have a steady platform from which to live your life.

That platform gives you the opportunity to deal with life and its seeming puzzles.

And, our part in life's plan is to trust the process and have faith, which requires only commitment on our part, nothing more. Commitment doesn't have to be difficult.

At this stage the only commitment required is to be open to the possibilities. One of those possibilities is that God will take care of it, that He'll help us work through whatever we're faced with.

Sometimes conflict within teaches us to be honest. It forces us to look inside. We have to decide whether we're ready to be honest with ourselves. Once we can be honest we are more in line with the spirit or soul within us. Our soul or spirit begins to have peace and can rest. Then we can stop being afraid of people not accepting us and accept ourselves. When we honestly accept ourselves, we can joyfully start living our truth.

Exercise

This exercise I developed for my clients who are in so much turmoil that they need simple, clear pictures, a road map, to see how they can start feeling better.

Take a piece of plain copy paper (the standard 8 1/2 by 11-inch size). Draw a huge circle that fills the paper. Draw a line down the center of the circle. Draw a line across the center of the paper. Label each quarter: Physical, Mental, Emotional, and Spiritual. In each quarter of the pie list three things that you can do to take care of each of these areas of your life.

For example:

In the Physical Health quarter:

- Number one might be exercise three times a week.
- Number two might be get at least eight hours of sleep a night.
- Number three might be eat a balanced diet and take a good multi-vitamin tablet with minerals.

In the Mental Health quarter:

- Number one might be to take a personal inventory of your thoughts throughout the day.
- Ask yourself are these healthy thoughts?
- Number two might be to keep a diary, which would give you a gauge of your thought processes.
- Number three might be to talk to a trusted, mentally healthy friend or counselor who can give honest feed-back on whether your thoughts are healthy or not.

In the Emotional Health quarter:

- Number one might be to make a list of 10 healthy feelings such as love, hope, joy and self-control. You can add more of your own feelings here. Please note that it is okay to add sadness and anger, which are healthy emotions as long as you don't get stuck there. When you have completed the list see how many of those feelings you had today. Were they used in a good way or did you get stuck? Are there areas you need to work on?
- Number two might be to record your feelings along with your thoughts in the diary. Again, this will help gauge where you are at today.
- Number three might be to review how the feelings match up with the thoughts, i.e., if someone has made you feel guilty (feeling) even though you know you have nothing to feel guilty about (thought). If your feelings and thoughts don't match, don't act on your feelings. The object here is to let go of a feeling that isn't true but pulls at you from your past emotional hurts. (A very important result comes from doing this part of the exercise: Good mental health is when thoughts and feelings match and your actions show that. In other words, your action is in line with your thoughts and feelings.)

In the Spiritual Health quarter:

- Number one might be to set aside 15-45 minutes to connect with God or your Higher Power by praying, meditating or reading inspirational material.
- Number two might be self-examination: Were you honest with yourself today? Are you living an honest life? In other words do you feel okay about the decisions you've made today? Are you feeling a little discomfort because of something you've done? If so, ask yourself how you could have done that better.
- Number three might be viewing the big picture. How are you treating others? Are you loving? Are you compassionate and understanding? Are you using self-control? Are you open to walking the spiritual walk?

I call this exercise the pie of life. It helps my clients see where they are out of balance in their lives and gives them focus — which leads to healing and a more balanced, peaceful life.

Prayer

Help us to be open to your goodness. Help us to be open to the possibilities that you offer. Help us to remove any fear we might feel about being open to those possibilities. Open our minds, our hearts, our eyes and ears to the knowledge of truth. Place our feet on the path to health and wholeness. *Amen.*

Dear Lord,
You are my light and my salvation
I ask that in my hardships you stand beside me and guide me
I am blessed. I thank you with all my heart.
I give my life to You and allow You to guide me down the path of life.
I love You. Thank You for Your loving guidance. Amen.

Love, Krystle
(Krystle Kalinyak)

Chapter 3

Faith Crisis...

Asking for an Open Mind

Before I go any further I have to address a concern I have for those reading this book. Some people may eat up the spiritual message here and beg for more. Others, who are new at this or who have had unpleasant religious experiences may be tempted to throw the book down at this point. What I ask is that those of you who feel uneasy try to keep an open mind about God's message of love. I ask that you "take what you like and leave the rest." If at some time in the future you are led back to take more, then that will be wonderful.

What am I talking about, you're asking. I'm talking about the fact that for me this book has to contain my entire spiritual experience. My spiritual experience is all about my relationship with God the Father and, yes, Jesus, His Son as well as my belief in the power of the Holy Spirit, whom Jesus called the Comforter. This relationship is the essence of God's message of love for me ... and for you, should you choose it.

So, I ask that you be at peace with what is coming and read on.

Wanting a Shield From Suffering

Here I was doing everything to know God and to come closer to Him and I thought I'd be shielded from suffering. After all He already had taken my most grievous pain away once. I was really upset that I lost that baby. It didn't seem fair and I thought God would play fair.

I needed the encouragement of those people around me who knew more about God than I did. So I started to ask questions. I wanted answers and I wanted them yesterday.

I remember them saying there are no answers, everybody goes through that. They would pray for me. Then they would say I should pray.

That didn't do anything. I couldn't pray, I was too angry. They kept telling me about this loving God but I didn't feel loved at that moment. So I retreated inside myself a little bit and I wondered about a lot of things. Most of all I wondered if I ever was going to have children. I was so sad. I was sad when I thought of the possibility of not having children. It was a challenge to me to continue to go to the Bible study, to pray with the people at work, and to go to the Re-New group. I felt like a total hypocrite: mad on the inside and smiling on the outside.

Not Living an Honest Life

I was not living an honest life before God. I didn't know it was okay to be angry with God. If you're going to have a relationship with God you're going to have all the feelings that go with relationships: love, anger, jealousy, sadness, happiness, patience, faith, doubt, passion — all those regular emotions. He knows who we are. We can't hide from Him or lie to Him.

So the truth was, I was mad. And we had to work through it together. Just like you get mad at your friends, you don't give up on them or walk away from them, I didn't give up on God and He didn't give up on me. I kept doing the things that led me to Him, hoping that I could make sense of my anger.

I was beginning to come to terms with what had happened. I still didn't understand it all but the pain was diminishing when within two months of losing my first baby I was pregnant again.

Talk about a roller coaster, emotionally, physically and spiritually. Not only were my hormones out of balance but

I was living in major fear of the same thing happening all over again.

This time the doctors monitored me closer than before. I started spotting and found I had a lack of one hormone and I had to take hormones through the first part of my pregnancy in order to keep the baby. I had to do this up through my fifth month.

In my fifth month I felt great. I felt secure for the first time. I felt life move within me. My anger was starting to dissipate. I started to get back that feeling of love toward God and thankfulness that I had made it through the worst of this pregnancy.

The ironic part was one doctor had given me a due date of Oct. 28. The other gave me a due date of Nov. 7. I remember looking to the heavens and saying as long "as it's not a girl on Halloween, it'll be okay." I was afraid if it was a girl born on Halloween, kids might pick on her and call her a witch. Sure enough, my baby girl was born on Halloween anyway and what I feared never came up, not once.

From the hour of her birth, I felt complete joy, more than I'd ever felt before. I remember looking at her precious little hand and the touch of her soft skin and her eyes looking up at me when I spoke. It was so awesome. You've heard the saying "some things are priceless?" That was a priceless moment.

Then I knew total complete joy. I quickly searched the scriptures to find just the right word of God to put on the thank you notes I sent for the many gifts we received. I wanted to show my gratefulness to God for this new life and His faithfulness to me. He had not given up on me even though I was mad in the beginning. He had stood by me and seen me through my crisis of faith. We truly felt blessed at the miracle of life through our new baby girl.

It was quite a spiritual experience. My faith was restored.

Mental Health and Spiritual Thoughts

There are moments we walk through darkness and we see no light in it. Those moments can be very black pieces of unforgiveness, anger, sadness, depression, hurt, loss, jealousy, uneasiness, guilt, shame or some other negative emotion. We don't see any light in those emotions.

During that time when I had been so angry, I couldn't see God's big picture and where I fit into it.

For you who are in darkness, light comes from just walking the steps in front of you even though you don't want to, even though it doesn't feel good. The feelings will never kill you — they just hurt pretty badly.

And through this all we don't know what's going to happen, where we're going to be. We just have to have faith that if we keep walking, and have hope, and look for the positive stepping stones in the darkness, we eventually walk out of it. We eventually begin to see a light. Before we know it we're looking back on the darkness from the light.

Some people have greater darkness to contend with than others do. They may have fatal diseases, murder, suicide or other major tragedies to contend with. But if they are willing and have the tiniest bit of courage they can open themselves up to the peace that comes from knowing God.

When you walk through tragedy with God or someone like a counselor or trusted person who offers acceptance, you begin to heal. The healing bond between two people can be so powerful that it verges on the holy. When someone takes the time to listen, when you feel like you've been heard, you begin to heal.

That's what it's all about, after all. We're here to represent God and to offer the qualities of God to each other: kindness, gentleness, love, forgiveness and patience. The best and most complete healing is divine. That's exactly what God offers -- acceptance, which is the balm of healing, and what makes healing so sacred.

There's hope in everything if you allow yourself to be open to God's love for you.

Exercise

If you are suffering from negative feelings such as unforgiveness, jealousy, anger, depression, ask yourself — what are the thoughts driving those feelings. This exercise will help you see not only what drives negative thoughts but will help you to stop thinking them. Obviously, it's not healthy to have negative thought patterns or the negative feelings derived from them.

List your negative thoughts. Examine these thoughts to see if they actually belong to you or to someone from your past who dumped their own garbage on you. In childhood it is very easy to absorb other people's emotional garbage. Unless you learn as an adult to throw the garbage away it will continue to be a part of your negative thought patterns.

Once you've made the list of negative thoughts, decide which thoughts are worth keeping and which need to be tossed out. The thoughts you think are worth keeping can be re-worded into positive thoughts.

For example, if you are feeling angry and depressed because you are taking care of everyone else's feeling before your own, you become resentful and bitter. To re-think in a positive way — think to yourself that your needs are also important. A positive thought process would be, "If I take care of my needs first, I'll have the energy to take care of my family and friends' needs." This example is not to be selfish but to learn how to take care of yourself and not be a victim.

The important thing to learn in this exercise is that your thoughts should work for you and not against you.

Prayer

Dear God,

Faith is something unseen. Help us to be open to the miracle of what faith can do. Sometimes believing is all that needs to happen. So we ask you today to give us that faith so that we can trust and believe in your love for us. Continue to restore us when we have doubts. Remind us that you are on our side. Let us feel your nurturing peace as we walk the steps of faith and give us the courage to keep going. Thank you for your acceptance and love. *Amen.*

Holy God,

You love me with more love than offered by all earthly fathers combined. Yet, for reasons I do not fully understand, I continually run away and get lost. I know Your delight is in giving me freedom; freedom for joy; freedom for life; freedom for love. Loving Father, thank You for always being there to welcome me home. A*m*en.

The Rev. Dr. Dabney T. Smith

(Episcopal priest)

Chapter 4

The Journey Begins. Who is this God?

When you take a journey you usually have to pack a suitcase to carry things you'll need along the way. In your walk with God the first thing you might want to pack is faith.

How did I get that faith? Where did I find it or a better question might be how did I learn to trust it.

Actually, I'm not sure.

I had made myself open to it but I know God had a lot more to do with it than I did. He provided the necessary ingredients. In this case it was first a healing from my deep grief, a loving family, my church community and then the miracle of birth and nurturing love for my children. I came to realize that if God loved me as much as I loved each of my babies then that was an awesome love.

I realized this soon after our daughter was born. I knew, but it was finally confirmed to me, that things like power and money weren't important; life was so much bigger than that. Her birth focused my attention on the journey of life. She was looking to me to journey with her and to be there for her. But my having to work was still a problem.

I wanted to be more available to her, to stay at home and spend more time with her. I asked Andy to go back to school and get a degree, so I could be a stay-at-home mom to help her in her journey in life and toward adulthood.

Andy went back to school and finished a four year degree in two and a half years. And I worked like crazy. The babysitter and my family watched our daughter while he was in school. When he was home studying, he watched her. I continued to work. I missed her and ached for her every day.

After Andy graduated, he was recruited to another part of the state and we moved. By then we had a second child, a boy.

I now had two children and finally got to be a stay-at-home mom. I found it was more difficult than I expected. But I did make one meaningful observation: children have wonderful, loving, accepting young spirits.

Looking at these little babies and the free spirits within them taught me about my relationship with God.

Our children put their total reliance on us and trust us as parents because they have nobody else at that point in their young lives. Their doing that generates an immense nurturing love within us.

For Andy and I to know these babies were a creation that came from our love, a part of our love together, just increased the love all the way around. And, I thought to myself, God's love is even more — it's infinite.

We are creations of a merciful God who wants only that we love Him as He loves us. It's like a parallel: our love for our children increases their love for us. And that love always is growing. So our love for God operates the same way. It constantly is increasing as we get to know Him more and appreciate the immensity of His love for us.

When I ask my clients what is their spiritual connection, most say they believe in God. But when they go to explain God they don't know who that is in their life. He's often very distant and far away from where they are at that moment, not touchable or tangible in any way. Some people refer to God as the Father, the Almighty, the Creator, the Alpha and Omega (Beginning and End), and the All in All but perhaps the easiest way for those who are unsure but seeking to know God and His Goodness is to think of Him as pure love.

His love is unconditional. He loves us no matter what. In our life's journey that's the most important thing we need to know and remember. That's what Christ is all about. Christ didn't care who you were, He loved you anyway and that's why God sent Him. God sent Jesus Christ, his Son, to show His compassionate love.

I don't believe God's love is conditional. He says that we always have the choice to accept Him or reject Him but He will always be there for us. We are the ones who make that decision. Of course, the closer we come to Him the more we want to be in line with His will for us instead of *our* will for us.

As a counselor I have found that when people live in line with His spirit of love (not necessarily in line with a particular religious dogma or set of rules) their lives are more peaceful, content and less dysfunctional. Can I explain that? No. It just is. It's part of the mystery. It works for me and for my clients who find their way to that path.

Interestingly, I've noticed that the clients who pray and grow spiritually seem to finish their therapy in record time. They seem to be more willing to drop the stuff, which is holding them back, and to move forward toward peace. It seems as if they have an extra source of strength, as indeed, I believe they do.

Unconditional Love

These clients have an extra source of strength because they have learned about God's unconditional love.

Here's a story of that unconditional love and acceptance as told in a parable by Jesus.

You know the story of the prodigal son: How the son of a rich man wanted all his inheritance early. He took it and spent it on youthful wild living. When he had no money left, he was forced to take a job as a lowly farmhand. While doing his job taking care of pigs, he concluded, that they eat better than I do. My father's servants have better food to eat than I do right now. So he decided to go back to his father, ask for forgiveness and to become one of his father's servants.

When he arrived, his father ran out to meet him. He accepted him with open arms, put a ring on his finger, a robe on his back, shoes on his feet and killed the fatted calf to celebrate his coming home even though he was totally undeserving of this kind of love. The prodigal son was completely welcomed.

In the same way we may not deserve the love of the Father but it's always there. We can't make sense of the Father's love, it just is. How many of us would have that kind of love for someone, who took our money, spent it unwisely and then came back? This describes the journey back to God.

John the Baptist was sent before Christ to help people turn back to God. He was there to help them examine the wrongdoings in their lives, admit their faults, tell God they were sorry and find their way back to His love.

The important emphasis here is on the "I'm sorry." It's hard for us, as humans, to say we're sorry or to admit wrongdoing. It also is hard for us, as humans, to forgive.

Unless we start to say we're sorry and to forgive others for their mistakes, there will not be any freedom in our lives. Staying in unforgiveness and wrongdoing keeps us at a distance from the peace that God offers.

Sometimes we have to admit we were wrong or that we made a mistake. We have to take responsibility for who we are.

Sometimes it also is hard to forgive those who either can't or won't ask for forgiveness, but we can do it anyway. God gives us the ability to forgive as we learn from making our own mistakes. Most often those mistakes come from not listening to your conscience or God.

Learning Through my Mistakes

Even as a mental health counselor who was living a spiritual life I had to learn to listen to what God was trying to tell me. I would come to know in time that this was the beginning of a lifelong process.

I already had received my master's degree and had my Florida license to be a mental health counselor. I was working at a center for counseling and addiction. I had plenty of clients and a following. My clients liked me. I began to think it was time to strike out on my own.

At first I went into a little office, I was all by myself most of the time and I didn't like it very much at all. I had no colleagues around me and it felt lonely.

But my practice was growing by leaps and bounds. I began to get enough of a reputation that a prestigious psychiatrist with an upscale office overlooking the ocean approached me and asked if I'd like to join his practice. His staff would handle all the appointment setting, insurance and everything that was an onerous chore to me. He said he'd help me build my practice even further. It was very tempting.

I felt flattered and I wanted to move ahead. My ego was stroked.

I started to ask everyone if I should do this. Most people said do what you need to do. But something inside me felt uneasy. I didn't *want* to recognize that unease of spirit as God's voice. It was too good an offer and my pride really wanted it.

So I did indeed pack my stuff up and away I went.

I ended up in a broom closet with a window overlooking the parking lot on the second floor. That office had dark brown, depressing fake paneling. All my clients hated coming there for some reason. Within two months I went from having a thriving practice to five clients a week, with a rent payment that was double what I paid before.

My stress level reached a peak. I had to work for another agency part-time just to make the rent on my "fancy" office overlooking the parking lot that I didn't like anyway.

For three months I agonized about what to do. My uneasiness continued. In fact, it grew. I knew it was time to take a step back and leave that practice to figure out what I would do next.

When I finally came to that decision — to step back — I had to say, "I'm sorry" to God for not listening. He had been telling me all along through my unease of spirit (I could call it my conscience) that the place wasn't right for me.

Soon after leaving, I met another mental health counselor through a friend. I had told her I was looking for a place and she invited me to come see her office. When I actually saw her building, I immediately felt peace. Again, God was talking to me. This time I listened. I've been there for several years now and I couldn't be happier. I came to know this is what God had in mind for me, but first I had to recognize I had gone against his guidance and I had to say, "I'm sorry."

Mental Health and Spiritual Thoughts

In my practice, many people come to me with problems that seem insurmountable. Some of these problems are created by other people, but the vast majority they have created for themselves.

I start to help them separate issues into what are theirs and what are someone else's — what's in their control and what's not. When that begins, sometimes as part of the healing process, we have to get to a place of forgiveness. I help my clients find the place where they need to ask for forgiveness and also the place where they have to forgive others and especially themselves. All of this is just like Jesus' parable of the prodigal son. The prodigal son had to ask for forgiveness and accept it.

And, here's a very important point. Many people who have received God's forgiveness can't forgive themselves, which causes blocks to their mental health, their healing and their closeness to God. They stay stuck. They can't come close to spiritual happiness because they don't feel worthy. They actually wallow in guilt. They're unhappy, they've asked for forgiveness and it's been given, but they don't accept it and therefore they stay stuck in a fragmented, unfocused place which leads nowhere and certainly does not hold spiritual peace.

This stuckness really is about not trusting. Learning to trust God can be difficult for those who never learned to trust. People find all sorts of real and crazy excuses not to trust: They may feel they are too smart and intellectual and God is a crutch. They may have been abused physically or emotionally and not trust anyone, much less God. They may even have a religious background that was very authoritarian and judgmental and so it pushed them away. There may be many reasons they have found not to trust. This is very sad — that any one of these things would keep God's children from his love.

In one way or another, this lack of trust leads to a place where they doubt themselves.

I wish I could say there is an easy solution to learning to trust. Starting with God is a good safe way to get there. Once you trust God, you can trust yourself and stop doubting yourself.

How do you do this? Just being open to starting, is a step in faith. First you have to be open to the possibility that trust and faith can make a change in your life.

In Alcoholics Anonymous, there's a premise that you surrender your will to something greater than you are, because up until this time your life has been unmanageable. Some people have trouble with this concept. They are so far from God that they have trouble using the word God and therefore they are asked in A.A. to substitute the words "Higher Power" when they surrender to something greater than themselves. If you are one of those people, you still can use those words "Higher Power" but the surrendering is the same as the step in faith and trust.

The only way to learn about trusting God is like getting in a pool: you can either hold your nose and plunge in or take your time getting wet. If you are the take-your-time type, each time you stick your little toe in you get a bit more trust. Pretty soon you can go in further, up to your ankle, then your knee, then you can be immersed and really feel God's unconditional love.

Here's a good way to begin. If you are seeking to learn more trust find someone whom you think is a safe person (i.e. a counselor, spiritual director, pastor or a friend who seems to be living a peaceful life) and talk to them, but carefully. Give them just little pieces at a time and see how it goes. If it goes well, keep going. If it doesn't, move on to someone else, until you find someone worthy of your trust.

Once you trust the person, it's easy to learn to trust God because the process is the same. So, in fact, you could start with God, if you want to get your feet wet or take the plunge.

Exercise

Give yourself 20 minutes for this prayerful meditation. Find a quiet place, read the 23rd Psalm and think about the still water. Feel your soul restored and feel God's mercy. And now go to a place of peace where you can feel God's love surrounding you. If you seem to be having trouble doing this, imagine yourself as a child crawling into His lap. Let Him hold you. Feel the forgiveness and peace He has to offer you. Just sit quietly, immersed in His love. Feel it's warmth, it's healing presence and unconditional nature. Keep the focus on God's love. Just be. When you are ready to come back to the here and now bring that sense of well being, which comes from God's love, with you.

Prayer

Dear God,

Help us to learn about your unconditional love through forgiving other people in our lives but most of all in forgiving ourselves. When we surrender, our heart opens and we become Yours. Teach us to trust You and give us the necessary faith to come back into Your peace.

We thank you for always loving us and forgiving us. *Amen*.

The darkness of my soul is illuminated when I once again surrender my will to God. Control, criticism, self-pity and fear do not overcome my circumstances. My battles are overcome by surrender, acceptance, gratitude and willingness to let go of my solutions. When I turn to God for guidance, peace and love light up my heart and my role in life becomes clear. I practice this process over and over.

Love, peace, blessings, angels singing in your ear,

Judith

(Judith Martinson, Licensed Mental Health Counselor)

Chapter 5

Playing Yo-Yo With God
The Emptiness

When you play yo-yo, you take the yo-yo and throw it outward but it's attached with a string and therefore you can make it come back to you. That's playing yo-yo. It's an ongoing away-and-back motion. That's how I used to handle my problems: I'd give them to God but I wouldn't cut the string. If God didn't take care of them fast enough or the way I wanted, I'd take them back again. Inevitably, when I took them back I'd make them much worse until they were unrepairable. Then I'd have to give them back again. I had to surrender and give them to God, because at that point I had made such a mess only He could fix it.

Praying with People of Different Faiths

While Andy was working on his degree in accounting, I was still working for the Telephone Company. That's where I met several Protestant prayers, as you might say, who really taught me how to pray.

I was searching and hungry, yet still very empty. The prayers and a bunch of other people like me would meet together at work every Wednesday for an ecumenical Bible study which included people from many different faiths. In this Bible study I met more than 20 inspirational people who knew God very deeply. I remember several of them saying, they wouldn't put their feet on the ground without saying a prayer as they woke— thanking God for the day — and I thought that was strange. I never met anybody who did that before.

I was just a bit in awe of them.

That kind of devotion to God and prayer was a very foreign concept to me. I usually thought of God only when I was in crisis. Only when I needed Him. Then I prayed without ceasing until my crisis ended. I never thought of God being there each day and everyday, all day long. That kind of concept, I thought, was only for the "holy rollers," religious groups who were scary in their devotion to God.

I was extremely fearful of turning into one of those "holy roller" people. (Interestingly, now my brother calls *me* one!) I didn't want to be thought of as a Jesus freak because of the ramifications I had felt on the other end of that. As a Roman Catholic I had met people who said I didn't believe in Jesus, which wasn't true, and I had felt judged and tossed aside like I didn't count. Even today this sometimes happens.

One morning recently as I had coffee and a bagel at a local donut shop I experienced this judgmental attitude once again. I had brought my prayer books and Bible in with me to read while I ate my breakfast. There was an older couple, probably in their seventies, sitting two booths down from me. They were smiling and winking at me as I looked up from my reading. When they were leaving, they stopped at my booth. The woman put her hand on my shoulder and said it was "so nice to see somebody reading the Word."

She proceeded to ask me what church I went to. When I announced that I went to a Catholic church the expression on her face changed drastically to one of great disappointment. She hurried back to her husband. He seemed just as disappointed and on the way out he spoke to me.

This is what he said, "Jesus loved even Saddam Hussein, so certainly there's hope for you" — putting me in the same category as this murderer and crazy man. I thought to myself then, "Blessed are the persecuted." At that moment I did what Jesus would have done, I turned the other cheek, but it wasn't easy.

Standing Together in Love

A concept which may be foreign to some extreme advocates of their own faith is that God loves all of us equally and knows that we, of different denominations, are all striving to come to Him. It hurts me for myself and for others, no matter what religious tradition — Methodist, Lutheran, Roman Catholic, Baptist, Episcopal, Church of God, Assemblies of God, Pentecostal to name a few — that people who profess to carry God's love, especially Christians, can choose to be judgmental in God's place. They cause division. And Jesus Christ, upon whom the Christian church is based, stood for love and acceptance. He ate, slept and lived with people who were just ordinary. Ordinary people who had sinned.

He condemned the religious leaders, the Sadducees and the Pharisees, who were more interested in petty rules than love. Yet today we have Christian leaders all around us who use their own sets of rules to judge (God's jurisdiction, not theirs) fellow Christians in much the same way that the Pharisees and Sadducees did 2,000 years ago. Instead of carrying Christ's main message of love, these extreme advocates of their own faith end up producing fear in their flock. They have lost sight of Christ's central message of love and hope and charity.

It's this kind of behavior that can lead people to play yo-yo with God. Because the God they've been taught about by, dare I say it, judgmental Christians, is not the loving, merciful God who fills all our needs and loves us unconditionally, but a God who keeps score.

In the Bible Jesus said, "Judge not, that ye be not judged." Judgment is not up to us. Jesus came here for the people who were hurting — for the sinners, for the sick, the lost sheep — to find them and save them.

Just remember that.

DIALING GOD'S CRISIS LINE, AGAIN

As I was saying, I only went to God in crisis. In my attempt to maintain control in my life and not surrender, I only found God useful when I needed Him. I remember thinking I didn't need to bother Him with the little stuff in my life. I really had no concept of an ongoing relationship with God. Here's an example, a story about that yo-yo approach. You will see how that kind of approach leaves one very needy and striving to control the pain and emptiness inside by controlling other people and situations.

My mother was 52, overweight, smoked, ate only unhealthy food and had a history of heart disease in her family. One day as she came to babysit my kids, she complained of indigestion which had kept her up all night. She said she had tried all those antacids and nothing was working. She had her arms folded across her chest still in pain. I called the pharmacist and asked if there was anything we could do for severe indigestion. He told me, "to hang up, dial 911. Your mother probably is having a heart attack."

As soon as I hung up the phone, my mother told me to do the same thing. She had gotten a blanket from my closet and was on her way back to lie down on my couch. She was a nurse and could sense herself going into shock.

Within four minutes, the paramedics were there. They administered oxygen and put her on a gurney. They hooked her up to the EKG machine and said that she clearly was having a heart attack. Then the paramedics told me they were taking her to the hospital and I was to follow behind. Panic set in. I ran to my neighbors and asked them to care for my children. I jumped in my car, hysterical to get to the emergency room. My father was a salesman and out on the road. Before I left I had called my brother who went to my parents' house and waited on the front steps for my father to come home. My father, sensing something was wrong, came home early and my brother was waiting for him.

There I was, sitting in that emergency room all by myself. I definitely felt alone. All I could think about was God and those people in my Bible study. I was praying non-stop.

An emergency room nurse came out to look for me. She asked my name and immediately I was scared my mother had died. When she handed me my mother's belongings I was *sure* my mother had died. My heart sank to the floor. But she told me they were still working on her.

Right after the nurse left, I went out to the phone booth and made a long-distance phone call (we lived in a different area code from my work place) to one of the people in my Bible study. I told her the situation and asked that she and my other Bible study friends pray for my mother, father brother and me and to pass the word to others to pray. I felt sure that would heal my mother more than anything else would.

I was in such a frantic state. My friend, Barbara, prayed with me right there on the phone.

It certainly calmed me down, and I returned to the emergency room. The nurse proceeded to tell me my mother was being transferred to intensive care. They said she was in critical condition and it would be touch and go. They couldn't promise me anything.

The emptiness I felt at that moment is beyond words. The next few days were a nightmare of not knowing. I slept on the intensive care waiting room floor and visited her as often as possible. When we finally returned home for a good night's sleep, my father, my brother and I were called back to the hospital. She had taken a turn for the worse. I remember being on my knees in the waiting room asking God to spare this best friend of mine. I told Him I would do whatever it took.

The Yo-Yo Begins

My prayers were answered. My mother was released in about two weeks. She came home full of promises that she would give up smoking, she would exercise, eat right and lose weight. And I came home to put God back on the shelf because He had done His job for me.

I was still searching and really did not know or understand the power of what had just happened. As I had dozens of times before, but never as strongly, I felt emptiness, a deep hole in my center. The hole yawned bigger than ever because this time I was dealing with the possibility of losing my mother.

Lots of my clients talk to me about the same kind of deep hole that I experienced then. Never feeling complete or at peace with themselves. Later I came to understand that God's love would, and could, fill the hole and there is no *one* else and no *thing* else that can fill that hole.

It's funny I wanted my mother to change her life. I wanted her to fulfill those promises but they only lasted six months. In my desperation to keep her alive for as long as possible, I began to be very controlling. I know that's kind of dysfunctional for a future therapist, but that's where I was.

I'd say, "Is that really good for you?" "Should you be smoking, now?" — like there was some way I had control over her destiny. Finally, in frustration, I gave it up in prayer during one of those work place Bible studies.

I said, "God, I can't live with this, thinking about it every single day, every single moment. Help me to cut the string to the yo-yo of control that I've been doing with you. So I ask for You to help me release this to You, once and for all."

After I prayed, I got an overwhelming sense of peace. I was searching for that peace because the doctors had told me chances were she wouldn't live five years if she didn't change her ways. I realized the future was inevitable and that I relied on her too heavily to fill that hole which I needed to let God fill. I began preparing myself to live a life without her by learning more about God.

But I didn't find the peace I was seeking until I actually let go of that yo-yo and started to trust.

Mental Health and Spiritual Thoughts

My clients, almost without fail, come to me out of a sense of needing to re-gain control in their lives. They truly believe that if they could just change the situation, or the other person, everything would be all right. They wonder why they're not listened to. They say the other person doesn't get it.

They never believe that they have a part in it.

They don't understand that if they see something differently or change their ways that the situation could change. They hang onto the need for control, believing that's the only way things will work out. Anybody who doesn't do it their way is not right, they think.

They may work several sessions trying to get me to say the other person/situation is bad and they are good. When I finally get them to realize that they are the only one sitting in my office which translates to they have to change, or let go — that's when the light begins to dawn. They begin to see that they must change before anything else really changes — such as an opportunity for happiness that they want but don't know how to get.

It's like taking them out of a tunnel and having them look globally at a situation. For one thing, there are more options globally. This becomes the turning point, really. They have to completely surrender and accept their part in making the mess they are in.

What they feel before surrender is emptiness and a struggle. They know they are miserable and things, try as they might, are not really in their control as they would like.

The truth is, things never are in our control and we are only fooling ourselves when we think they are or think we can have control over everything. Real life just doesn't work that way and certainly happy, spiritual life does not include control over other people and situations.

True happiness comes from connection with our soul. And our soul is connected to God.

People actually believe that things or people are going to make them happy. It's not so. That leads to a whole other type of yo-yo lifestyle. While a person, situation or thing could possibly make you ecstatic for the moment, inevitably there is the drop off where that person or thing is no longer making you happy as you once were. And you're off again looking for a new source of happiness.

True happiness does not yo-yo. True happiness is about gentle peace in your life. Peace comes from the connection between you and your soul and ultimately between you and your Creator. Having that connection fills the emptiness inside, fills the hole of fear and gives one the ability to live authentically; the ability to know your true values and live them which leads to good self-esteem and confidence. When you have both good self-esteem and confidence you don't need to look for happiness in all the wrong places.

Connection comes from knowing God is there for you, each and every moment. He's there when you pray, He's there when you are in church, He's there when you're eating, when you're driving, when you're sleeping, when you are afraid, when you are lonely, when you are sad and when you are happy. He never, ever leaves. (There are those who doubt that God is present in bad situations but He still is there. When God sent Jesus, He never promised to end the suffering, only that he would be there in it with us — to spiritually hold our hand through life, to comfort us and carry us through the bad times and the good times too.)

Remember that: He never, ever leaves. He's there for all of us, each one of us.

Exercise

Ask yourself: what are you controlling and why? If you can't see anything that you are controlling, try asking what things in your life are bothering you the most. Make a list. These are the areas you need to focus on and begin letting go.

Once you make the list, you have recognized the problem areas in your life. Control is about being in the middle of, and trying to fix, the situations that bother you the most. Ultimately, control ends up controlling you. You have to step away or out of the situation to allow people to have their own natural consequences.

A possible example: At dinnertime every night your spouse and son argue. You jump in and try to make peace. You get indigestion and irritated and they're fine. Next time this happens take your plate and go to another room to eat without saying a word. The results will be totally different.

Your final part of the exercise is to get up and leave the situation that most bothers you or that you are trying to control. But you need to warn your family members, or the people in the situation, that in the future you will be leaving when their behavior starts affecting you.

PLEASE NOTE: *What I'm recommending here refer to everyday bothersome situations, not the big life-changing issues such as marriage, sickness, death or occupational issues*. For these bigger issues, consider counseling with a professional. These bigger issues do not easily go away and the fastest way to heal them is through God, counseling and prayer.

Prayer

Heavenly Father,

Thank you for your love and presence. Help me to learn the joy and peace that comes with surrender. Help me to learn to release my burdens a little bit at a time, until I trust you with my entire life. Help me to be willing to let go and try something new. Change can be scary, but with your merciful tenderness, I know I can do anything. Give me the courage to take your hand and move on. *Amen.*

Heavenly Father,

We thank you and praise You, that You are alive and ever present. Help us to see You all around us. Give us the desire to look for You, the awareness to notice, the heart to receive you, and the boldness to share what we see. *Amen.*

Love, Debbie

(Deborah Vann, Licensed Clinical Social Worker)

Chapter 6

My Small Significant Signs The Power of God

The power of God leaves me in awe. Here is one of my most incredible stories of the power of God in action.

In the summer of 1998, my family and I were in Gatlinburg, Tennessee on vacation. We were planning a trip that day to Dollywood. Because it was really early, around eight in the morning, my husband Andy had poured himself a big traveling mug of coffee. As we started on our way in our van down the mountain roads, he took a turn and the coffee which was on the dash rolled onto the floor. He leaned down to get the coffee and suddenly the van was no longer on the road.

"Oh my God," I said, "Andy, look out..."

When he looked up, he saw we were in dire trouble. We already had gone over the edge of the mountain road. We were in the trees headed toward the bottom of an exceedingly steep slope. We were sliding sideways through the trees and picking up momentum when, somehow Andy stopped the van. But we weren't out of trouble yet.

We were looking straight down a terrible incline and, at first couldn't see how it was possible we had been able to stop. The kids, ages 11 and 14, were hysterical and crying.

Once the van stopped, we seemed to be suspended in air. The van had come to rest on a mere twig but we didn't know then what was holding us.

"Nobody move," Andy said.

Now the kids were *really* crying.

I started to pray. "Lord we're all ready to come to you but if you want us to stay, please send us somebody."

At that *very* moment a man, seemingly straight from God, tapped on the window.

"Is everyone alright?" he asked.

We could only see his head because we were that far off the ground. He went around the van to see if it was alright for us to get out. Then he told Andy to get out of the van. Andy had to jump out onto the ground. Then my son dashed over the seat into his arms as fast as he could. By this time a human chain of people had been formed and they passed my son up the chain, about 100 yards, to the top of the mountain where we had left the road.

My daughter was next but she was paralyzed with fear. So I slowly talked her up front, where she jumped into her father's arms and they passed her up to the road also.

Now, it was my turn. They were worried about me getting out because the front of the van was dangling over the precipice and they were afraid if I moved it would start the sliding process all over again before I could get out.

But carefully I edged my way to the other side of the van and was pulled to safety by the people in the chain.

Everybody made his or her way back up the mountain. By this time the police and fire-rescue were there and they had called a tow truck for the van. The tow truck driver got the van out with little effort and there was just a dent on the door. I remember paying the tow truck driver $65 and we were off to Dollywood for the day.

Now that's the awesome power of God and prayer.

Open 24 Hours

While in the middle of this traumatic experience God

answered our prayer right away, but it is not always this immediate. It may take time and patience before some prayers are answered and sometimes He doesn't answer in the way we want or expect but, even in this process of waiting, we are often granted God's peace and grace to keep walking.

And, He's all around us. We don't have to live life alone. We can talk to Him any time we want, night or day, he's always open — 24 hours a day.

He'll take care of your life as long as you invite Him to. He's not an intrusive God. He will only come if He's invited.

So if you're lonely remember God is with you.

That's what makes us appreciate Him — that out of all the millions of people praying to Him, He can still hear each of us and take care of each of us individually.

In the Bible Jesus says "all of you that are burdened, come and I will give you rest."

I believe what He means is we can always ask Him to take charge, to make the decision — but we have to ask. I counsel people everyday who say they believe in God but then when I ask, "What does that mean to you?" — they don't have a clue.

What I've found is that God is not up in the sky or far away, but someone who walks right beside you and is as close as the breath that you breathe.

People who work for hospices say, "All we ever need to do is just breath." What they mean is don't make life complicated or worry about what is going to happen to you.

We're here one day and gone the next. Life is fleeting. And the amount of energy that we spend in chaos and worry and despair is not worth one moment — especially when you can have a life (and have it abundantly) of golden moments with God. That's what Jesus meant when He said in the book of Matthew, "Thy kingdom come thy will be done on earth as it is in heaven." You can have golden moments of heaven right here on earth just by surrendering to His nurturing guidance.

His loving companionship and power are available to you here, right now.

God has been there for me all of my life but that doesn't mean I knew it.

After my mother started to heal from her heart attack I began to relax my vigilance in my relationship to God. After all, she was back with us and for a while I didn't need him, I thought.

From that day under the altar I had started a relationship with God, but now things were a bit different. During major moments of crisis I have prayed for myself and those I loved. I had opened up the floodgates of my heart and the connection between God and me was strengthened.

I had prayed and He had answered my prayers, all of them — even saying no at times. I started to be aware of His presence in my life every single day. Everything I prayed for, He answered as if He wanted me to know that He was there. I felt like He was pleasing me instead of me pleasing Him. Instead of feeling emptiness I began to feel Him everywhere.

People in the Bible study used to say to me there's no such thing as coincidence — it's just God — God-incidence. For the first time I was beginning to notice that what they said was true.

God-Incidences: Signs of God's Love

Here are some examples from that time:

I was married in the early 1980s when inflation had driven interest rates up to eighteen percent on mortgages. We were in a contract to buy a house, but that kind of interest rate made it impossible. The house was so tiny, only nine hundred square feet. Once the interest rate got to eighteen percent, our contract fell through. We were living with my parents, which was not ideal for anyone, especially with us being newlyweds.

I prayed and talked to God about our situation. Doing that — talking to God — was very unusual for me because I never had thought about talking to Him about everything. Before I just talked to Him about the really serious stuff, the life and death sort of things.

Within a week of my beginning to pray for a change in our living situation, my mother came home from grocery shopping and said she had seen a notice on a pizza parlor window about houses that were "spec" homes that had interest rates of ten percent. She brought me the phone number. I said that was impossible, there was no such thing in this inflation market, but I'd call anyway. I thought she had read it wrong. Within twenty-four hours I was standing in what would be my first house and it was much better than the other house we were going to buy — much better than we had anticipated being able to have.

My mom had gotten better from her heart attack and my prayer was that she would be around to know my children. And she now was better and would live several years more.

A simple one: One month we were really struggling —we could hardly pay our bills — and I got a check from the insurance company — just showed up — a refund from something we had changed. It was totally unexpected. I had prayed, "Please God, help me find a way to pay this," and sure enough that check showed up.

During that same time Andy had gone back to school and I was going to get to stay home soon. It just seemed like God was in charge — all I had to do was trust and follow and it would be fine.

I kept thinking this was much easier — learning to trust

and follow, praying and keeping my eyes open for His answers — than trying to run my own life or trying to decide what was good for me. I felt like He had rolled out the red carpet to show me that life didn't have to be complicated, that I made it complicated.

Up until this time when God showed me life didn't have to be complicated, I felt like I had controlled my own life, that I made my decisions all by myself. I thought I was in control but I sure noticed it took a lot out of me and produced a lot of anxiety, even despair. It took a lot to keep going under my own steam.

There's that thing in 12-step groups about surrendering your life and will over to a power greater than yourself. That was exactly where I was. I was learning to turn my life over to God. The relief was immense. When I remembered to pray first, it always seemed to give me a greater sense of direction. He always had answers I could not have thought of — even on a good day.

But His thoughts are not our thoughts.

I believe He has the whole picture. When we come up against obstacles we might have just a piece of the puzzle. If we just plow ahead instead of going to Him — things can get worse instead of better. When we seek Him, we are granted His peace and resolution. Sometimes we don't even have to make a decision. He takes care of it before we even have to worry about it.

So, I've learned to sit and wait on God.

Sitting and waiting on God seems to be something this culture knows nothing about. In the moment when I'm in distress and waiting for signs from God, I realize the truth of the saying "patience is a virtue."

We moved from our first house, the "God-incidence" spec home, when Andy took a job on Florida's East Coast. As the children began to get older he started to hint around about my going back to work.

Whenever my thoughts went there, to the idea of doing accounting again, total dread washed over me. I couldn't do it anymore. I knew I couldn't. So I had been thinking about what I could do instead. What was I good at? What did I like? After prayer, the only thing I really came up with was that I was good with people.

Someone that I worked part-time with encouraged me to look into the counseling field.

It sounded good to me. I took the Miller Analogies Test to get into the counseling program at Rollins College in Winter Park, Florida. I failed that test twice. I stunk as an analogist. So I thought to myself, maybe that's not what I'm supposed to do. I had mentioned to my sister-in-law, who was not usually interested in my job-related stuff that I was looking into this field.

The strangest thing happened. One day as I was waiting for the mail to get the results of my second try at the MAT, there was a letter in there from her. Inside the envelope was a newspaper clipping for a master's degree program in counseling from Nova Southeastern University out of Ft. Lauderdale, Fl. That university had just started an extension at our local community college for working people to get their master's in counseling. The greatest revelation about this was I didn't have to take a test. I was bad at testing to begin with. Here, all I had to do was pass the first four classes with an A or B.

I passed them with A's and they matriculated me into the program and I was on my way to becoming a counselor, loving every minute of it. But it took some time before I could see God's plan for me in this process. I had to read the small significant signs He put in my path.

Here's a story from a fellow counselor about one of God's small significant signs for her:

A couple of years ago she heard the words "conversion and transformation" everywhere she went: from friends, in books and from family members. It didn't make any sense to her, although she now realizes she was in the process of conversion and transformation at that very time. Coincidentally, or God-incidentally, she picked up a book she had for almost 20 years and never read, written by noted British author and theologian C. S. Lewis. It was, naturally—a story about conversion and transformation.

The book is *Surprised By Joy.* It's an autobiography and the end of the book is about his conversion to Christianity.

As my friend and fellow counselor told me, "I was reading the last page where he talks about the final step of his conversion which happened when he was on the way to the zoo. It was too coincidental," my friend told me, "because later that very day I was planning to take my son to the Jacksonville Zoo. It was one of those coincidences that really gets your attention."

As I said before I had noticed these God-incidences myself.

What I noticed about this was that God was doing the same thing with her that he did with me: showing her all these "small significant signs." She would call me on a daily basis and tell me all her God things, every single day. It had been, and was, the same for me.

She would say to me that I was sent to her to affirm all her God-incidences. I did for her what that Bible study at my old job had done for me.

Recognizing Those Small Significant Signs

Pay attention.

Live a conscious life.

Take time to notice when things are flowing well and what significance that might have. When you start to recognize Him around you, you start to see how often He's there for you and takes care of things. Simple little things, like having just the right amount of time needed for a project; things being settled before you have to make a decision about them; getting home before your car dies or just having enough cereal and milk to make it through till you can get to the grocery store. These are simple things that we just take for granted. They are little blessings to be noted.

When seemingly surprising good news arrives on your doorstep and it is like an unbelievable coincidence that you were just talking about, or praying to God about, and suddenly there is your good-news answer — that's one of those small significant signs.

A friend of mine was terribly overworked and burdened with her job as a free-lance writer. She needed money and had taken on a ton of work which she finished in a miraculous three days — but all the time she was talking to God asking for help — asking for writing work that was easier, less intensive, paid more and would be more to her liking. Only half an hour after she finished her last deadline and was almost crying with the pain in her hands from all that writing, she got a phone call. The phone call was from an editor of an upscale magazine asking her to do work on just the type of subject she loved. It meant a lot more money for much easier work. She had been talking to God. She believed in God and her prayers had been answered. She gave the glory to God by telling all her friends. To her, that phone call was one of those small significant signs — showing that God is present all the time, mercifully hearing our prayers and loving us.

Here's another small significant sign.

The other day when I walked into one of my sessions my client said, "I'm so glad you moved my session. I had been praying all day long because I had such a busy day planned and it was going to be so hard to make the session and when you moved it up everything fell in place."

She paused and looked thoughtful. "It must have been God," she said.

As we made our next appointment, she said she wasn't sure about the time but she would just pray about it, if the time was wrong. And then she said she was sure God would take care of it.

These are examples of simple signs from God. Prayers are always answered, however they are not always answered the way we want them to be, or think they should. Some will be answered with a no. Keep an open heart. Recognize every small significant sign along the way. The journey is a process and sometimes it takes time and learning to trust that God is in control.

When God Says No

God sometimes says "no" to a prayer and when He does there can be a good result from that "no." Sometimes people don't realize till afterwards how grateful they should be that God said no. Here's a good example of a blessed "no" given to a friend of mine, Amanda, an administrator in her church.

"The Stephen Ministry, which exists in many denominations, assists people in need. It's a care-giving ministry. I wanted to work in the Stephen ministry. But before you can begin the six-month's training they interview you in your home. So my husband and I were expecting an interview on a particular Tuesday night.

"But that morning we had to go to the church office for something. The man who was in charge of the Stephen Ministry came out and said he was so glad to see me — that I should go talk to the two women who were scheduling the meeting that night. When I did, the women told me that although they had advertised Thursday nights as the time for the training sessions, they had decided to switch to Saturdays and do two sessions in one day.

"I told them that I had school on Saturdays (I was in a Christian studies program) but I was a quick learner and probably could make up the lessons. They said maybe that was possible but then they mentioned they might be doing other Saturdays as well. In my earnestness to be a Stephen Minister I told them if they did the sessions on the second and fourth Saturday I still could attend, because my classes met on the first and third Saturdays.

They said that, unfortunately, they had planned on meeting on the first and third Saturday. I looked at them and said, "I can't do that."

They told me it had to be my decision. I said, "there is no decision." I got up quickly and left the room before they could see me cry, because I felt very, very rejected.

"My Christian studies program had first priority. I knew I was being called to the ministry but I didn't know what kind of ministry. I thought all these classes would make me a better teacher for Bible studies. I already had a year invested at this point.

"When I got to the car I was feeling rejected, hurt and disappointed. I was angry, too. I slammed my hand on the steering wheel. I asked God, "Why don't you want me to be a Stephen Minister and serve your people?"

"Later, I felt like God was telling me that I would serve His people, but I wanted outward validation as well as inward validation.

"Soon after, I had lunch with a friend, the Dean of the Institute for Christian Studies where I was taking my classes, and the whole gist of the conversation was to see if I was coming back the next year. He told me he believed I was being called to be a deacon. I realize now the reason God closed the door to the Stephen Ministry was because He was calling me to an ordained ministry where He could use me to minister in a larger area which included the healing ministry — physical, emotional, spiritual healing — as well as prayer ministry.

"Eventually, I became a hospice chaplain, in addition to preaching and teaching."

Today, Amanda says she is not an evangelist but a missionary. She leads healing and teaching conferences at other churches in all denominations throughout the United States. She's doing God's work on a larger basis and reaches more people than she ever thought possible when she sought to do one ministry within one denomination. She says, "That was God's gift. I came to realize that in ministering to others, I am the one who is blessed."

But there is an addendum to this story that is as important as the story itself.

Amanda found she had to work hard to forgive the man who headed the Stephen Ministry: Not only had he made the schedule so inflexible she couldn't join, but he also never invited her husband who also had expressed an interest in becoming a Stephen Minister.

Two years went by and for some reason she was led to hand the man a brochure about an upcoming, two-day healing and teaching conference. She suggested he come and he did.

Amanda explained, "His wife was going to drop him off there but she decided to stay. That night we had a healing service and I was paired with the bishop when the man came up for healing prayer. I put my hand on his heart when we started to pray. The bishop's prayer was to have his heart beat according to the Creator's plan.

"Later that evening several friends came to my classroom to talk and share a birthday cake. This man was there and started asking me many questions about Jesus. We went and sat in a corner and I had a long conversation with him, which to this day I have not shared. Finally, it was almost midnight and I told him we'd be there tomorrow and we could continue talking then."

But it was such a pretty night and Amanda was so energized by all the prayer and conversation that she wasn't at all sleepy. She asked her conference roommate to take a walk with her.

"The sky was so beautiful," Amanda said. "I threw back my head and arms and looked toward heaven. 'What a great night to die. When I die I want it to be on a night like this and feeling like this' — that's what I told my conference roommate.

"We finally went to bed and around 2 a.m. there was frantic knocking on our door. It was this man's wife saying "come quickly, I can't wake my husband up." I had just received a cell phone as a gift from my husband that very morning so I dialed 911 as I threw a sweatshirt over my pajamas. We ran across the compound to where they were staying. We immediately realized that God had called this man home. A little bit later we took his wife out of the room and stayed with her until about 5:30 a.m. — by that time the funeral home personnel were there to get him.

"The wife, who had not cried at all, said she wanted to see him one more time. He was on a gurney and covered with a sheet. When I made her request known they removed the covering from his head so she could see his face. Then she started crying. She said she could see the Glory of the Lord all over him. So I've always felt that the Lord's healing which took place that last evening gave him time to find peace and me the opportunity to help him. I feel death is the doorway to the ultimate healing because that's when we come face to face with God."

Mental Health and Spiritual Thoughts

If you are living in discontentment it's much harder to see God's small significant signs and to hear God's message of love, mercy and hope for you.

As to the BIG significant signs — the awesome powerful signs -- don't worry, you won't have any trouble seeing those. Christians often talk about being hit between the eyes with a spiritual two-by-four. What they are talking about is a sign so large in their lives that they can't help but pay attention.

But it's the small significant signs that often let us know God is with us. However, it's not always easy to see the smaller signs if your life is out of balance.

When you live out of balance — doing things that everybody knows are wrong, including you — you may be deceiving yourself that your life is alright. But is it? Are you truly happy and at peace? When you live out of balance with God, things can get very complicated and difficult. You become discontented and it's like a pit that you fall into and can't crawl out of without help.

God will speak to us in the wilderness. He's there, calling us to live in harmony. If you find yourself overwhelmed and struggling with the ups and downs in your life, you might want to ask yourself, "What am I so consumed with that I can't see my way?"

Small significant signs can give us the opportunity to notice God's blessings. What they add up to is a solidifying of our faith. We recognize that our prayers are answered, that God is present everywhere in our lives.

When you recognize one small significant sign, you'll start to see them everywhere and they are such joyful, happy blessings because what they mean, after all, is that we are loved.

There are times when people walk into my office and things look so gloomy, so dark to them that they see no way out. They can't see that they are loved. One thing I constantly tell my clients is that you have to recognize what is good in your life, even if its just the sun shining or the rain feeding the grass. I say you have to stir some light — some positiveness — into the darkness.

I teach them to write a list of five to ten things that they're grateful for and if they can't think of them they have to ask their best friend, spouse or someone in their life what they need to be grateful for. Then, I tell them to post that list on their bathroom mirror and look at themselves in the mirror and say what they are grateful for on that list, out loud, everyday for at least six months.

During that process they begin to see there really are things to be grateful for and this alone can lighten their load and give them some relief. I tell them, "By doing this you re-record some of the negative memory that has been handed to you all of your life. You get to stop the old memory and start a new one, sort of like 'it's time to change the disk.' "

This boosts my clients' self-esteem. The process harkens back to the psychological theory that if you change the thought, eventually the feeling changes, not right away but after a while. Then your actions reflect your new thoughts and feelings. That's truly good mental health: when positive thoughts match positive feelings, which produce positive actions.

In counseling, change normally doesn't take place for six to nine months. So I tell my clients they have to continue and be diligent about saying the list of things to be grateful for. When they do this, it helps the counseling process. Everything speeds up and they get better much faster than they would otherwise.

The list of things to be grateful for, very simply, combats the doom and gloom.

Exercise

Take a few moments now and make a gratitude list of five to ten things, or more. Learn to appreciate the grace-filled moments of your life. There are always so many, just pay attention.

(You may have been so sad or depressed you think there isn't anything to put on your list. You may even have gone in your thoughts to the concentration camps and said, now what could they have been grateful for? Well, a man named Victor Frankel wrote a book about that very subject. You know what he was grateful for? That the guards couldn't destroy his inner being... his spirit. He never gave up hope and he survived the war.)

Prayer

Dear God,

We come to You with great thanksgiving for the simple beauty that is all around us. We ask You now to help us to see beyond our darkness into the light and love that You have provided for us. Let us never underestimate Your awesome power and Your immense love that You share with us every day. Give us clear vision to see those small significant signs in our daily routine as we journey together. *Amen.*

Heavenly Father,

Open my eyes to see and ears to hear. Help me to recognize those who, you Father, have chosen to come into my life, for whatever the purpose, however long the season. Teach me, so that I may become a saint for the ones who will cross my path...in Jesus' name. *Amen.*

Love, Lori

Lori Claro

(Teacher's Assistant)

Chapter 7

When the Saints Come Marching In

I believe God basically sends us people throughout our whole life. Looking back there were several people sent to be on my path that I would call teachers. I still am receiving teachers to this very day. The teachers in my life right now are Barbara, Hazel and Debbie. We are learning together and are in the process of founding a ministry of healing. They are the latest in a long line of teachers.

My first teachers were teachers of the Word, teachers of prayer, teachers with knowledge to impart about a loving Savior. Each one fed me what I needed at that particular moment in time — as if God knew the menu that I required for finding spiritual grace.

Let me introduce you to some of those people whom I was fortunate and blessed to have come into my life just when I needed them. As an adult, the first teachers I had came to me through my workplace, the telephone company. But I also have to give my mother credit; she gave me my first knowledge of a loving God.

First Teachers

Here are some of those teachers and what they did for me.

Barbara and Sylvia: At break time I'd often see them outside, giggling or close together in a quiet stance. I was attracted to their smiles, joy and a quality of peace that they seemed to carry with them.

I wanted what they had.

My best friend had been murdered two years previously and God had miraculously healed me of the pain from that loss, but I was still spiritually hungry and wanted to know more.

The only thing I can remember is that at break times when I needed prayer they'd meet me downstairs and outside in a grassy area. They'd take my hands lovingly and say the most beautiful prayers. I felt like they really cared and they knew something special. As a Catholic, I had never before heard ordinary people pray out loud. It was very comforting and their faith was evident in their actions. Our religions were different but I trusted their prayers.

They encouraged me to pray and they built me up spiritually. They taught me the power of prayer. And they stood with me together in that prayer and offered entrance into the Christian community. They urged me to become more active in my church so I could be fed spiritually there as well as with them. And what I found was the Re-New group.

And in marched Peggy. She was the third person to offer Christian community to me. She was the leader of my Re-New group. Andy and I were the youngest couple in the group, by nearly half a century. Talk about wisdom. It was like a direct line of nourishment from those who had been through the ups and downs of life. These people knew the Lord deeply and shared His love with us. We spent many hours around the table discussing scripture and life.

Spiritually, I had been starving and now I felt fed and I knew there was more where that came from. We went to that group for about a year and then the group broke up when Peggy died. That was a sad time for all of us.

My next teacher was a girl I had overheard talking at work. I was surprised to find out she was an Assembly of God minister's wife. She lived in my town, which was about 45 minutes from work. This seemed to be another God-incidence. She taught praise aerobics. It was great! I needed some exercise. It was the best aerobics class I ever attended. I had never thought of God as fun, but that was fun. Her name was Renee. She taught me to love the Lord with joy.

Our aerobics class would start simply with prayer then we would do aerobics to praise and worship music. We sang hymns and got the best workout of our lives. I was starting to see that God wasn't just so serious. I was high on life in the Spirit. Renee was a vibrant, exciting person. She didn't preach doom and gloom, but peace and joy. She preached a living God that was present for all of us and wanted us to have the desires of our hearts and to *be glad in Him* who had created us. Because of her, we knew we were never alone, He was there for us. He always is there for us. I had to give up the class when I got pregnant with my daughter.

Next Dottie marched in. She was part of my Bible study at work. She must have seen how hungry I was. She brought her spiritual books in, one by one, so I could read and learn more about God and life in the Spirit. Often we would eat lunch together so I could discuss the books that she had loaned me. She seemed so willing and open to talking about anything. That was an exciting growing time for me.

Some March On

As quickly as they had appeared, these teachers — I call them my "saints" — suddenly marched out of my life. I found that I was learning, praying and studying on my own and mostly within the confines of the church. My children were young and I was homebound, so for a while I was learning about God all by myself. And, frankly, I wasn't very good at it without the support.

Then, five years later, my mother died and I was in extreme need all over again. The grief was overwhelming. God and I were talking a lot more than we had in a long time. Way ahead of me, my God of infinite love knew my needs. Just when I needed support the most, He surrounded me with people who also had lost their mother. I didn't recognize this though, until she died.

Teachers for Every Occasion (Including Grief)

There was Margaret, with whom I worked. She was much older and provided much love and comfort for me during this time.

There was my friend Pennie, who spent an hour on the phone each week listening to me cry and talk about my mother. When I wound down, she'd say, "Okay, I'll call you next week and check on you."

That meant everything to me. She threw me a life preserver when I most needed one. She was very compassionate, loving and understanding.

My Aunt Barbara would call me two or three times a week from New York to check on me. She is my mother's sister. She provided a safe place to go for the Christmas holidays when they loomed so empty ahead of us. She was very spiritual and her nurturing reminded me that God is a loving, nurturing God.

I learned that all you really need to do for people who are grieving is listen with a loving ear and heart.

The strange thing is I had all these good friends and yet, during this time, I didn't really hear from any of them. I remember asking why hadn't any of them called and one said, "What would I say to you, how could I even comfort you?"

Apparently, these were not the people whom God chose to work through. Pennie, on the other hand, was just an acquaintance and Margaret was a co-worker, yet they understood loss of this magnitude. They showed God's compassion and helped heal me back to life.

After I began to heal from the grief, with help from these new saints, my spiritual learning went quiet again for a while. Not too many people were there, but I had grown closer to God than ever. I had become attached to Him.

In the meantime, I was finishing up my master's degree and I had promised God as soon as I got out of school I would start to work in His church in some way. I wanted to give back what He had given me which was extreme comfort during two very sad and troubling times in my life — times when I physically ached with the depth of painful emotion I was feeling.

Saints of the Present

When I began volunteering at church, a myriad number of "saints" marched into my life.

One very helpful teacher was Melissa. She became my spiritual director some years after I moved with my family to Florida's East Coast.

She taught me how to be quiet and listen to God, that He was present with me in my everyday life, and that I didn't have to go on a search for Him. She taught me all I had to do was be still and know He was there for me to feel His presence. She's the person I return to when I have spiritual quandaries.

There are many other people I work and pray with at the church who have been and still are teachers to me. These people have been put in my path for me to grow in love, peace, gentleness and kindness — all of which Christ teaches. They all have had a great impact on my life and represent the true presence of God.

Which leads me to my most recent "saints," Barbara, Hazel and Debbie. They are my prayer partners who meet with me every week to pray. I am so blessed to be in their company. Barbara is a Roman Catholic Christian evangelist and author of five books on healing, who travels all over the country to speak to people about God's healing love. She is a founding member of an international organization, The Association of Christian Therapists. She is president and founder of the non-profit group, Be-Loved Ministry Inc.

Hazel is a deacon in the Episcopal Church. She heads up a healing ministry, the International Order of St. Luke the Physician for the entire southeastern region of the United States. She also speaks and teaches the message of God's healing love.

Debbie is another Christian counselor who has been counseling for 18 years. We work together. Debbie, an Episcopalian, does volunteer work at her church in several areas including bringing adults to Christ. She and I both knew Barbara. She introduced Barbara and me to Hazel.

In other words God brought us all together.

Now the four of us, in addition to praying together weekly, have formed a ministry for the purpose of teaching, healing and "ministering to the ministers." I can't tell you the incredible joy, peace and healing which takes place when we pray together.

We formed the ministry to "minister to the ministers" because often they are so weary from serving in the Christian community. We came to realize that we could help them just by praying for them, so we do.

We also have monthly, open-to-anyone evening healing services in a church about 20 minutes from my house.

Those are my saints. I believe everybody has saints who come marching into their lives — they just have to open their eyes to find them. Have you found *your* saints?

Mental Health and Spiritual Thoughts

When we are in emotional pain, it's hard to see anything good in our life. It wasn't until just a few years ago that I began to see that certain people in my life, modern day saints, represented a pattern of God reaching out to me — of God showing me His mercy and nurturing. Sometimes when we can't see the forest for the trees we can't quite figure out who those saints might be.

People, even our own modern day saints, can sometimes — because of their humanness — disappoint us, but in my experience God never does.

When we need to have situations dealt with for our mental and spiritual health as well as our general well-being, we can always go to God.

One of my saints taught me a meditative exercise for going to God with our concerns. It doesn't matter how you go to God but I find this exercise helpful.

Exercise

The exercise that was given to me was not one of prayer petition as much as prayer listening. I pray meditatively. I close my eyes in a quiet room with no distractions and I envision the situation in my mind. Then I ask Jesus to reveal Himself to me in it. I sit quietly.

Sometimes it takes a long while for Him to show up and one wonders what's keeping Him. My personal take on this is that it is very important to clear the air. If there is unforgiveness in your heart release it to God. Surrender it. This always has worked for me.

Just by example, here is one such occurrence when He showed up.

In addition to private practice, I used to work for two mental health agencies. At one of them, I had an unfriendly boss who was very abrupt when questioning me about my work skills, often leaving me with a lot of hurt feelings. He would point his finger at me while being very critical which was degrading. If I hadn't had lots of good self-esteem and believed in myself, I probably would have felt humiliated.

As it was, I felt like I received a punch in the stomach each time he went on a tirade. At the height of his attacks I began to feel like the situation was more than I could handle. One night when I went home feeling hurt and discouraged, I remembered I wasn't alone that I could bring Jesus into the situation. After all, He's much bigger and He loves us both, then and now.

When the meditation started, I was in the office being belittled by my boss. I was hurting. Jesus appeared in the doorway and He had such a loving look for me, with such loving eyes. He came over took my hand and led me out of the building all the way to the parking lot. He said to me, "No more hurt. We have work to do."

After that I felt freed. I no longer work there. What freedom, what joy!

For me, this exercise has been one of the most powerful in my life. When you come up against life's most difficult circumstances — ask God to shed light on your situation in prayerful meditation.

When things are beyond your human control or you feel your weakness as a human being, Jesus Christ is the one to call on. Try this exercise, you just might find you can't ever again live without it.

Prayer

Thank you God for loving us so much that you send extraordinary people to share our pain, sorrows and joys. Thank you for sending Jesus Christ who loves us back into life and who is in every one of us. We are broken, so broken. It is with these people in our life and with Your help that we can begin our path back to You and wholeness. Help us to deeply recognize Your Son in everyone we meet. Teach us to be saints for one another, to share the unity of your love. We ask all of this in Your Son's name, Jesus Christ. *Amen.*

Lord God,

From the beginning You have always been in relationship with me. In my heart You have placed a desire to be in relationship with You. May I have the grace to always respond "yes" to your initiative within me. *Amen.*

In peace,
Father Leo
(Father Leo Hodges, Roman Catholic priest)

Chapter 8

My Relationship Begins

"What a friend we have in Jesus..." old hymn.

People act as if their relationship with Jesus is different and set apart and indeed, it is, but it also is similar to the relationships we have in our everyday lives.

When I first started noticing Jesus, after my friend Pat died, my relationship with Him was pretty new. He was an acquaintance. I knew of Him because I grew up with Him. It was like I had been introduced to a friend of my mother's, but I never really got to know Him.

At that time, He was very far away. I thought of Him as living up in the clouds in heaven. I certainly didn't know that He could be my close friend. I thought I'd meet Him someday when I died.

I didn't understand the concept that I could have a relationship with Him right now.

Like any relationship, I had to get to know Him. Certainly, He was there when I was rescued from the pain when Pat was murdered and for me that was a good starting place. I remember thinking: Wow! That was pretty remarkable. I thought if prayer—just talking to Jesus could do that—how much more could He spiritually enrich my life? And what was I missing by not talking to Him more?

My spiritual hunger came from those questions. I was on a search, a mission to meet Jesus and learn more about Him. I started thinking about all the times He had reached out to me, through my friends the modern day "saints," through my sufferings and solaces and in my joys. I began to see that He was everywhere: in my marriage, in my children, in my church, in my workplace, at the supermarket — He was everywhere. And I began to welcome His friendship and be more attentive to it.

There's an old saying, "to get a friend you have to be one" — that's how it was for me. I began to see that I needed to be a friend to Jesus as He was being to me, that it is a two-way street. The more I put into the friendship, the more I got out of it.

But I also felt like the Lord placed a desire in my heart that was so immense that it wasn't a choice any longer. He became the source of my energy. He filled all the hungry and empty spaces in my heart and entire being. Now remember I'm telling you this after 22 years of walking on this path. I went through the same ups and downs with my Lord, Jesus, which I had with everybody else.

A personal relationship is not born overnight. It is hard work, like every relationship in our life. It takes our time, our energy, our attention but most of all it takes love. Our relationship with Jesus is no different.

In the beginning of relationships we test the waters. We test loyalty by sharing some personal information about ourselves and by asking for help in situations. We look to see if we can trust and depend on that relationship.

Remember that when relationships begin they're really great — I call it the honeymoon stage — when you're sort of goo-goo eyed over each other. Just everything goes really wonderfully: You are overly nice, on your best behavior and you say all the right things.

For me, it was just like that with Jesus. He was *there* for me. He answered my prayers as if they were direct-line radio requests and He was listening to everything I said without a doubt. And, I was hanging on to every word and constantly aware of His presence. It was the best time.

I was drawn to Him more and more. That lasted for quite a while.

And then things started to go wrong. Things like my mother having a heart attack, miscarrying my first baby and having a devastating fight with my mother-in-law that ended in an absence of communication for many months. In all of these I felt powerless and helpless to help myself and started to get angry and drift away from Jesus.

I wanted to know where He had been when these things happened. Somehow I thought He had left. I was angry. I thought if I had this great relationship with Him, He would continue to rescue me and I wouldn't have to feel anything but goodness. It was almost like I was alone in the desert and nobody knew I was out there by myself. I felt abandoned.

But, I somehow felt it was my turn, that He was testing my faithfulness to see if I really was His friend as He had been mine.

He was particularly quiet during that time. It was hard for me to maintain my faith. I didn't understand. I thought maybe getting angry with Him made Him go away, but I wasn't giving up. I knew He was out there, but He seemed to disappear off my radarscope. I couldn't just use my direct radio request line, as I had been. I went looking for my friend Jesus because I missed Him.

He had stuck by me and I was going to stick by Him. So I continued to pray and talk to my "living saints," those people who had brought me to Him in the first place.

Still, I got very discouraged when I didn't hear from Him for a long time. I started to doubt and have fears again. But I hung in there anyway because I had hope. After everything I'd been through and had come to know, I believed that eventually He'd hear my prayers. The thing is, that in my heart of hearts, I knew He really *was* there. He just seemed so far away again.

I realize now I was so consumed with the things that were happening in my life, worldly things, that I put barriers between me and Him — which made it hard to see He was still there.

Unfortunately, the same sort of thing happened with Andy and me, later on in our marriage.

We seemed to have hit a wall where communication was not as good as it used to be. I was sad because I loved Andy and wanted us both to be happy. After 20 years, I can say marriage brings lots of ups and downs. Marriage takes work from both partners. And there were times when I might not have gotten through the downs if not for the refuge that I found with God.

When Andy and I stopped communicating we drifted apart. I started to spend more time away from the house because it was easier to communicate with my friends. There was a lot of tension in my household. It was hard for me to be at home. It was hard for Andy, too. It seemed like we stopped caring and he could see that I was drifting away from him.

It came to a head one Saturday, like it had so many other times over the years. Only this time, it went from being a problem to a crisis when we decided the only answer was to separate. We wanted to see if there was anything left between us and we promised each other to work on the marriage and ourselves during this time.

We did what I would advise any couple to do in these circumstances. We got marriage counseling and went to a Christian marriage program. Both worked wonders and Andy and I are grateful for what we learned about each other and our relationship. I just didn't give up hope and neither did he. Both of us worked really hard on communicating and now things are better.

Good communication is the key factor in good relationships.

The willingness to listen produces good communication. Listening is an art. They say the best of listeners only listen 30 percent of the time. So, most of us are only being heard about 10 percent of the time. That's the reality and it leaves a lot of people in pain.

So many people are starving to be heard. Maybe you are one of them. Maybe you are so sad about your relationships, about a parent dying or a cherished pet and you have no one who hears you. You can feel pretty empty and alone.

I know when I heard Pat had been murdered it took the wind right out of me. For the longest time I wanted to talk about it but it seemed like no one really wanted to listen. Not being able to spill my guts about something so devastating led to my depression. I kept cramming in the sadness and fell deeper and deeper into the pit of despair until that day when God heard me.

Now, He's the first one, and the last one, I communicate with. This is not to replace having conversations with those who are important to us, our family, friends, co-workers and the people we meet day in and day out. I no longer feel as if I don't have anybody to talk to, because I know there is God. I talk. He listens. He talks. I listen.

Listening takes discipline. It takes a clear mind and the ability to repeat what the other person said, word for word. Listening is not forming answers while the other person's talking. It's an unselfish act of love. It is the act of *presence* for the other person. Your relationships will be so much richer if you practice this on a regular basis.

Still, in my relationship with Jesus I found He listens the

best — not 30 percent of the time, or 50 percent, but 100 percent of the time. You can always count on Him to hear your joy, your grief, your sadness, your needs, and even your anger. He listens to it all because He loves us into life — that is the real life in the Spirit, where we can find peace and even joy.

Mental Health and Spiritual Thoughts

My clients — when they first come in -- are so consumed with their stuff and so overwhelmed that they notice very little about my office. I can always tell they are getting better when they begin to notice things. That shows me that they have reached a good turning point. Whereas before, their problems had been consuming them, now, when their problems have stopped consuming them, they are able to see more clearly and notice other things around them.

That's a good checkpoint for most people.

If life is consuming you and it's hard to think about anything else but what's going on, it's time to do something. Go talk to a trusted somebody. Or start a journal. If you can't find anyone who will listen. Talk to Jesus. He will hear you.

How do you know He hears you? Just think about all the near misses in your life. All the times something good has happened for you, whether it's big or small.

In an earlier chapter I talked about a gratitude list. This is why you make one, for your mental health and spiritual welfare. A gratitude list will give you better perspective. There is much more to life than what consumes you. Look around. Be aware. God is present in everything.

For goodness sake, ask His help for you to have a wider vision and openness. Ask God to send you answers. They're probably right in front of you. Don't give up. Remember He's in charge. He can do more than we could ever think possible.

In my practice I don't mention my spiritual beliefs unless my clients bring them up. If they mention spiritual beliefs, pro or con, I help them explore those beliefs and feelings. Many times if I'm led, I ask if I can pray with them.

However, no matter what, I ask God to help every single one of my clients, especially the ones who are having the most difficulties. Those clients, just like heart attack patients who are prayed for, all seem to receive grace and an opening to the healing process. I believe that grace and that opening come from prayer. If a client adds their own prayer to mine, the results are even better. Every time I pray for a client who is in dire straits, something happens that is good. It's always very positive; they move forward in their therapy and mental health. And that's how I continue to know Jesus listens to me and hears my prayers. That's what having faith in the relationship with Jesus and God is all about.

Exercise

Exercise 1:

Practice listening by taking 20 minutes a day with a friend, co-worker, your spouse, your child or even a salesperson. Allow them to talk and repeat back to them what they said. You start by saying, "I hear you saying"... and then say what you heard. Sometimes you'll find that's not what they said and you will have the opportunity to clarify their message. But if you've really heard them, they will respond positively.

Exercise 2:

Start an Answered Prayer Journal. Write down things that are bothering you, things you need answers for, or prayers for those you love. Pray about them and give them to God. Once a month go back and review your prayers. Write down the ones that have been answered, how they were answered and how you feel about that. Give thanks to

God for hearing you. This is a good practice for the rest of your life and you will be amazed at how God hears your requests — and the sometimes creative ways He answers them.

Most of all this Answered Prayer Journal provides hope, even when prayers seem unanswered. Over time you will begin to see how strong the communication between you and God really is. It will convince you that God is listening.

Need help putting together a prayer? Here's the prayer I usually pray for my clients. You can pray this prayer too, for those who you think need it. Or, change the words a bit and pray it for yourself.

Prayer

Heavenly Father,

Thank you for everyone you send into my path. Make me a clear instrument for your light to flow through me — that this person would see You and not me; would hear You and not me, would know You and Your love through me. After all, You are the Almighty Healer, the Great Counselor and the Loving Comforter who sent the Prince of Peace. And You can do so much more than I could ever do, so help me to be present and send Your angels to minister to this person and to me. If any darkness surrounding this person comes before us, we ask You to come against it and remove that darkness forever. I thank You for hearing this prayer which I ask in Jesus' name. *Amen*.

Father God Lover of Life
Creator Redeemer Sanctifier
You fashioned me in my mother's womb, You gave me life, You cared.
You redeemed me from my many sins, You freed me, You care
I heard the word "Metanoia" — "turn around and follow me."
How, I ask?
And You answered...
"Just look for me, take time to see, listen with your heart
"For then you will learn how to live and give life
"And be at peace in your heart."
Open my eyes Lord, I want to see, open my heart Lord,
Teach me your ways, your truth and your life
I want you to come into my heart.

With love from, Melissa

(Melissa McKenna, spiritual director)

CHAPTER 9

God Is Everywhere: The Fruit of the Spirit

God *is* everywhere: in our family members, our friends, our work places, our churches, our activities. He created the grass, the trees, the oceans, the sky, the stars, sun and moon and all of the living creatures. I heard someone famous once say that they came to believe in God, because when they asked the question who or what could have done all this creating — the only possible answer *was* God.

Because we're so busy in our lives, we've moved away from enjoying everything around us and especially from taking time to enjoy creation. Life is busy. It usually keeps us going from very early in the morning to very late at night. And it's really hard to find time for God, unless you want to.

The question here is about readiness: are you ready to move from a materialistic lifestyle to living a spiritual life? With our cell phones, answering machines, voice mail, laptops, sport utility vehicles, soccer-parent time, grocery shopping, boss-pleasing, power-oriented, money seeking and possession-dominated lives, we hardly seem to have time for the simple pleasures that God offers.

After all, God isn't calling to you from the television set — telling you to buy Him with lip-smacking pictures of hamburgers, fried chicken, pizza and candy. He isn't trying to sell you a life in the spirit along with a car. He doesn't rip at your emotions with violent or pornographic movies.

He just is.

He calls to you in the silence. You must be willing to hear Him and turn down the volume of your life to recognize His presence.

Seriously, when was the last time you stopped to smell the roses and I mean literally? When was the last time you noticed the dew on the grass, the flight of a butterfly or the mercy of Jesus?

Stuff Will Not Bring You Happiness

The more meaningful parts of life are the simple things like holding a baby for the first time, a hug from someone who loves you unconditionally, a comforting word when you need it, a dog's tail wagging at your presence, or a proud moment when someone you love accomplishes something such as graduating from high school or when someone says they're sorry for hurting you. These have lasting effects on the quality of your life. They don't come with warranties because they don't need to. When you die, these precious moments of your life remain with the people you love.

And when you die, most of the stuff that can break, gets old looking, or stubs your toe, just gets sold or given away.

When my mother died, we had to sell the house because my father couldn't afford to live there by himself and we wanted to move him closer to us. She had accumulated a lifetime of stuff that filled the garage from wall to wall. It took my brother and me hours and hours to dig through that garage — to dig through all her clothes — and to give away furniture to the Salvation Army. All my brother and I kept were silly things. He took a picture off the wall of a lion that my mother loved. I took her glasses that were around her neck, her key chain and her cigarette case. Those were the things that were important to us as her children, mementos of who she was.

What was more important was the legacy of the love she

had given us. By comforting us when things were not okay. By sharing in our joy. By always being gentle and kind to everyone she met. That's something she instilled in both of us. Some things are just priceless. The God-things are priceless. She lives on in me, not because of stuff, but because of her love that she shared in her life with me. Now, I share that love with my children, my family and my friends.

Love is What Remains After You Die

Here's my question: Will the love *you* share with those around you live on in them after you die?

My next question is: How do you let go of the need for things -- your attachment to the stuff that swallows up your time and life and instead find a life of peace where you can share your love freely?

You might be asking — how do I begin?

You begin by noticing God. By recognizing bit by bit His nurturing love in His creation. By looking for Him in the loving actions of others and by mirroring that love to everyone else you meet. By prayer. By being aware — making a conscious effort to see Him and to recognize the fruits that come to you by walking on the path of wholeness, which He offers.

I've already told you about the "modern-day saints," people who brought knowledge of God and Jesus Christ into my life. I've told you about how my own life has been healed. For me, good change came when I began to see His hand in leading me to peace.

I began to see a pattern of grace that was giving me a life of balance and serenity. But before that every time something went wrong in my life, I would worry about it nonstop. I would try to figure it out and try to fix it knowing all along that I could just say a prayer. But I didn't think about that at first.

It would take so much energy, completely drain me before I would figure out I could surrender and give it to God.

There's a famous saying, -- "Let Go, Let God." For me, I came to realize the anxiety I was experiencing was never worth even one moment of my life.

I was healed of that anxiety in a special healing service. While attending a conference of the Association of Christian Therapists, I went to a service where several people prayed over me. When I left that service, just as when I left that church years ago without the burden of depression over my friend's murder, I no longer had anxiety about anything.

Now I live my life in trust. I can honestly tell you that I am experiencing the fruit of peace more than I have in my entire existence. I came to realize that if I leave things alone and I pray that everything just seems to work out and I don't have to worry about it. Sometimes, doing nothing about a situation is the best answer. Now I can keep that peace even during anxious moments and times of trial, something I used to think impossible. But all things are possible with God.

Some people that I know say I have the gift of faith. I believe that over the years I've grown into faith — grown into accepting the peace that faith brings. I've learned that faith comes from seeing God work in your life. But you have to make time for Him, just like you make time for everybody and everything else.

Mental Health and Spiritual Thoughts

When you want to make a change in your life you have to make a choice to live differently and that means a change of attitude. It's similar to healing from an illness, you have to rest and take your medicine.

So when you welcome God into your life, you have to do your part to enjoy the benefits of His Grace and then you become blessed with the fruits of the Spirit.

Wherever Jesus was in his ministry, He healed. He brought joy and hope and grace. He set people free from their brokenness. He wanted to provide for people's needs and desires. And 2,000 years later, He still does.

He came to set us free — free from ourselves.

The fruits of the Spirit are the characteristics of who Jesus Christ really is. So, of course, it's something to work towards. All of us would like those fruits of love, joy, peace, patience, kindness, generosity, faithfulness, gentleness and self-control, but we're human and we're not perfect.

We are a work in progress. So, the best we can do is remember what Jesus stood for in His earthly life. For us to love the person in front of us, to live and share in the joy of others, to be peaceful, to have patience, kindness and generosity to be faithful, to treat all creation with gentleness and to practice self-control.

That's the best we can do. But if we live according to the fruits of the Spirit, we will receive the benefits of those fruits.

For instance, if you deal with an angry person by giving anger back, it just produces more anger. If you deal with an angry person by offering love, you have a better chance of resolving the anger. That leads you back to peace.

Aspiring to the fruits of the Spirit leads you to the rewards of balance and serenity.

Exercise

It's important to have quiet time in your life for balance and serenity. This is the exercise I use seek out God and you can, too. Find meditative time. I have an hour of prayer time everyday, before the rest of the family gets up. In my prayer time, I say certain special prayers for the world. I pray for things that are going on in my life. I pray for my family, my friends, my clients and any special requests that I have been asked to pray for. I read devotional books with daily readings and a scripture reading from the Bible along with a commentary about that scripture. Then I close my eyes and ask God to allow me to come and sit in His presence quietly. As I ponder over the things I need to do each day, I gently bring myself back into His presence by saying a spiritual word to re-focus (such as peace, forgiveness, mercy, Jesus, Lord) — whatever word works to bring me back to the presence of God. I do that for 20 minutes. I set a timer to make sure I don't go over. Sometimes, God bless me, I fall asleep which I think is fine because He's still working on me. (During the day I also continue to pray when things come up.) That's it.

Make time for this kind of spiritual connection with God; you'll see the results by becoming more peaceful.

Prayer

Dear God,

Thank you for Your presence in everyday life. Open my eyes Lord so that I might see You in all of creation. Open my ears Lord, so that I might hear Your voice gently speaking to me. But most of all Lord, open my heart, so that I might love more deeply and have the lasting fruit of Your Spirit, which leads to serenity and balance. Help me Lord to do all things for Your glory. In Jesus' name we pray. *Amen.*

It is when you believe in, and trust yourself implicitly, that you will discover; allow yourself to receive and truly experience your very own Gifts, Dreams and Miracles.

I'm so proud of you. Love, Pennie
(Pennie Mills, Licensed Massage Therapist)

Chapter 10

My Gifts and Talents Are Discovered

I had a lot to overcome from my childhood including learning disabilities and financial insecurity. As an adult I added spiritual reluctance and job dissatisfaction to the list. But I had come to know the Lord and was ready to be a servant. I wanted to share my peace and hope with others. Was I in for a surprise when I found out what God wanted me to do!

I had grown up in a household where there had always been money problems. My parents married young. One had grown up in a poor household and the other had grown up in a fairly wealthy household. To say the least, they knew nothing about handling money. And, this influenced both my brother and me throughout our whole lives. I think somewhere we made a pact with ourselves that we would never struggle with money problems like our parents had.

My father had an eighth-grade education and was determined to see that we got to college, but we still had to pay our own way. He wanted us to have an easier life than he did.

When I was a teenager, he and I discussed possible careers for me. I wanted to go into some sort of criminal psychology. My father diligently searched for something that would say this career field paid nothing. In his eyes, money was the object in choosing a career. He knew that I was good in math, somewhat, so he directed me into a business administration major with a minor in accounting.

There was money in that field, but also a lot of emptiness for me.

EVEN THOUGH YOU'RE GOOD AT SOMETHING, IT MAY NOT BE THE PLACE TO WHICH GOD IS CALLING YOU.

While I worked at the telephone company as a clerk, I also was working on my degree. I had dreams of working my way up to manager eventually. And I did. After I graduated from college, I immediately got a promotion. Two years later I became the manager I had dreamed of being.

I hated every minute of it.

I could not see doing this for the rest of my life. It didn't even motivate my little toe to want to get up in the morning and go to work. Deep inside, I knew I had picked the wrong career. I knew I had picked the wrong thing but I stayed just long enough to have my children under the benefits package, and for Andy to graduate from college.

Upon his graduation, a Fortune 500 company on Florida's East Coast recruited Andy as an accountant. That meant I could quit the job I thoroughly disliked and stay home with my sweet babies. But as they were getting older and headed toward kindergarten, Andy started asking when I was going back to work. The mere thought made me sick to my stomach. It started me searching for something else where I might grow. I thought about counseling. I had always loved people so I started to volunteer for a local teen pregnancy shelter and also for a teen runaway shelter.

I was basically checking to see if I really liked being with kids that had problems. I found I really did enjoy it.

However, that wasn't the only indication I might be good at counseling. I sometimes felt like I had a neon sign on my forehead that said, "you can talk to me," because everybody did.

But the thought of returning to school was tremendously frightening. I had grown up with learning disabilities which were undetected and I spent the first year at my community college working on building skills to overcome those disabilities. I had been blessed the first time around by getting a four-year degree.

It scared me to death to think of getting a master's degree in anything, let alone counseling. I can only say the desire that God placed in my heart was much bigger than my fear. I had never been good at tests and I had to take a test to get into graduate school.

After taking it twice and failing it twice, I thought maybe that wasn't what God wanted me to do.

But there was another school and this school made you pass the first four courses with an A or B to be matriculated into the program. I knew I could do that, so I went for it. It was just what I was looking for. I loved every minute of it. I believed it was finally going to be the answer to the emptiness in my career life.

Before I graduated I had to do two internships. One was in an agency that was operated like a private practice and the other was a private practice.

It seemed to me that my supervisors were sent directly from God. Not only did they know their stuff and how to help people resolve their issues but also they were kind, supportive and encouraging. I felt like I was finally on my way and doing what I was led to do by God. I no longer had that emptiness. I began to feel job satisfaction for the first time in my life which, in turn, meant I was feeling peace and fulfillment. I felt connected to God in this field. It definitely was a spiritual experience, doing counseling.

The funny thing is that most people say, "How can you do that job? It's so draining," or "How can you listen to people's problems all day long?" But instead of feeling drained I felt energized. I don't quite understand it myself — all I know is when you're hooked up with God there is a living source of energy that doesn't end.

So Thankful

I was so thankful to finally feel the contentment of completing school, passing all my tests and finally getting my license that I wanted to give back to God what He had given to me. So, out of my gratefulness I started to do ministry at my church. First, I became a Eucharistic minister, meaning I helped serve Communion. Then, Andy and I volunteered to be the leading couple for a small Christian community, a group of people from church who get together regularly to study scripture, to pray, socialize and be there for each other. The small Christian community lasted about three years.

Not only did Andy and I grow spiritually during this time, but I also learned an interesting God-fact; as soon as you get comfortable in what you are doing in ministry someone will come and ask you to do something else that needs to be done. Once I realized this, I could see it operating in all areas of my life. I have come to believe that this is the way God helps us to grow. It even says in the Bible, "And he said to them, 'Pay attention to what you hear, the measure you give will be the measure you get and still more will be given you.' ".

After three years in that small Christian community, our pastor came to us and asked us to begin to lead a new project in the church. He said it would be a big job but he thought that it would change the spiritual tone of the church or, as he put it, "evangelize" the church. It was a retreat process given over one weekend. At the retreat people share their personal testimonies on spiritual topics.

It was exciting and new. And yes, we have seen people completely transformed from this process. There was one man at the retreat who didn't even go to church, now he goes every Sunday. It's such a healing process.

Andy and I are so amazed at what God does during these retreats. We just open the doors and He floods in. Man, is it a flood! We do a retreat every six months and people in the church give them. What we always see is healing of mind, body and spirit.

Out of one of these retreats, one person was so inspired that she started a prayer meeting with song, scripture reading and laying on of hands and she invited Andy and me to attend. Earlier while doing the retreat process she and I had talked about the power of the laying on of hands, which I had learned about some years before.

Later, in the prayer group which got its beginnings at the retreat, people were regularly asking me to pray with those who particularly needed prayer. I felt like I was being drawn into what I had envisioned years before, a healing ministry. I didn't know what that meant, but I was ready for what God was ready to give me. I now trusted Him fully. And today, even though I occasionally still have these human doubts deep in my heart, I really know everything will be alright because of my experience of Him.

I had felt the call for nearly six years to go into the healing ministry. I always felt counseling was a healing ministry, so I thought I was already there.

But, I even had a dream I would be doing talks on healing and spiritual wholeness. I kept hearing the word "healing" over and over. It's sort of the way God speaks to me. So I began to think maybe even more was being asked of me.

A Piece of the Puzzle

Over the years of my growing in spirituality, I had learned that God gives you a piece of the puzzle, one piece at a time. You just have to be open to walk the mystery. You don't have to understand everything when God asks you or places a desire in your heart. He provides the way.

Because I kept hearing that "healing" word so often, I ended up going to a healing prayer service in Orlando with two of my friends. After the service the deacon from that church met with us. He looked me straight in the eyes and said, "And you will walk by them and they will be healed."

Jesus Christ teaches that through His power we are given gifts to use in His name and to glorify His purpose here on earth. Of course, what the deacon meant was that I would be able to call on Jesus to help heal those who needed it. (I don't want to get into teaching or preaching here but there is a difference between fruits of the spirit and gifts. Gifts include healing and fruits were discussed in the last chapter.)

I was surprised. I asked him to repeat what he said, so I could know if I really heard what I thought I heard. And he said it again.

I walked out with the thought, "I wonder what that was all about."

The next thing I knew I was doing healing services with Barbara Shlemon Ryan, one of my "saints" who was placed in my life and whom I mentioned earlier. She has been in the healing ministry for 35 years.

And that's how I came to write this book. Because, first, God got my attention by saying "healing" over and over. And then I started hearing "heal my people." At first, I thought, that's what I was doing, but He let me know He wanted a book written that could reach more people.

Mental Health and Spiritual Thoughts

John 8:32 in the Bible states that, "And you will know the truth and the truth will make you free."

Jesus proclaimed this scripture and it's so right.

So many people when they first enter therapy are so far from their truth. They come in confused, searching and definitely in discontentment. They spend the first three sessions sorting through the muck. That's how I describe it — the muck.

They're not sure what they really believe or why they believe it. So often we go small piece by piece to figure out what they truly value and why they were unhappy enough to come for therapy. For instance, they'll say their husband says this about them or their wife says that about them, or a brother, sister, parent, child or friend says something about them. Then I'll ask, "Do you agree with that?" Sometimes I'll get a yes, but very often I get a no. And a statement, "They don't even know who I am."

It's obvious no one has heard them.

That's precisely what we work on. Who are you? Under all those messages that you grew up believing and still believe ... who are you? We talk about what messages work in your life and what messages bring distress.

What do you believe apart from your mother, your father, your spouse, your boss, your best friend and your children? What do you believe and what do you value in life?

Examining these messages is primarily necessary for you to get to your genuine authentic self.

Clients often tell me I am the first person in their lives that they could trust. I believe that ability to be trusted comes from my attempt at living an honest and authentic life.

As you can see from reading this book, the biggest gift that I have received is the gift of a loving God and a God who loves me so much that He gives me the opportunity to talk about Him freely anywhere. What I do and what I am flows from Him.

Here's the wonderful part of this: God loves you as much as He loves me. All that He has offered me He also offers you.

Here's the sad part of the human condition: We are born into this world in truth and we spend our life covering up that truth, undoing everything God sent us into the world with.

This is what I mean when I say we spend our lives covering up that truth: Babies are born with spirits of truth but can grow-up in environments where they receive all kinds of yucky, negative messages that remove them from that spiritual innocence. That's what happens to all of us.

And then, when we get overloaded, we need help. In therapy, we start to do an inventory and begin to peel those negative messages off layer by layer, back to that spiritual innocence. When you peel the layers you get back to who you were intended to be in the beginning.

Sometimes, it's important to first acknowledge you were given the negative messages.

Then you have to acknowledge that it wasn't yours. All of us carry around a backpack of stuff we try to get rid of by passing it on to somebody else.

Sometimes we get our parents junk or our grandparents junk—junk from past generations. For instance people say, "You're just like your father." Depending on who your father is that could be a likeable statement or not. The truth is, you are a special, unique person created by God and you have gifts and talents that were meant just for you, to be used to help and serve others around you.

One of the things we teach in therapy, Christian, spiritual or secular, is what those gifts and talents are, and how you can best use them. When you get to a gift that's especially right for you, it becomes a source of energy. Your talent may be gourmet cooking, bicycling long distance, praying for others, working with the less fortunate, being an honest accountant or being a mental health counselor.

Whatever it is, it will feed your soul, not starve it.

When you get to your truth you stop doing and start being.

When you are unhappy you become very busy creating things in your life to consume you because you don't want to stop and think and feel the bad feelings. When you are satisfied with your life and living truthfully, you stop running and start living.

Exercise

Living an authentic life comes from prioritizing your values.

List your top five values. Put them in order of priority. Now take an honest look at these values. Then make a comparative list of where you spend your time, talent and money this week. How did you do? Are you really living an authentic life according to your values?

This is how I now order my life:

1. God
2. Marriage and Family
3. Church and being part of a Christian community.
4. Friends
5. Work

If you really believe in your values, then you want to live in accordance with them. That's what I say and what I work towards with my clients. I share with my clients that nobody's perfect but I do know when I live these values in an authentic way I have contentment.

To work toward authentic living and attain contentment continue this exercise once a week. Notice where you are spending your money, time and talent. Is it in line with those things you value most?

Prayer

Dear God,

Thank you for creating us all individually special. Thank you for loving us all individually and for granting us gifts that are uniquely from You to us. You send us into the world in truth and light and we become bogged down by our humanness. Help us to find our way back to the created, authentic and spiritual person that You meant us to be. Help us to peel off the things that are not from You to be replaced by the characteristics of Your son Jesus so that we might live in peace and harmony every day in our present life. In Jesus' name we pray. *Amen*.

Dear God,

Please open my heart and mind to Your love so that it is only Your healing power that flows through me. Give me the words that others need to hear and allow me to be a channel for Your divine plan. You have created all of us in Your image and You want us to be whole and healthy. Please help us to remove anything that interferes with our true state of wellness. Thank you God for all of your blessings. Amen.

We are all one, Jill

Jill Todd, Licensed Clinical Social Worker

Chapter 11

Healing - The Call

Luke 9:2 in the Bible states that, "And he sent them out to proclaim the Kingdom of God and to heal."

The Whisper of God

For six years, I heard God whispering the word "healing" in my spiritual ear. What I mean is that I kept feeling deep in my heart that the healing ministry was something I was supposed to do. When God places something in your heart, He doesn't stop until you grasp the message.

People who have not experienced God whispering in their spiritual ear may have a bit of trouble understanding what I mean here. The best way I can describe this process is that spiritual and loving thoughts come which speak of His presence all around you. These are spiritual thoughts that you would not think about on your own.

For instance, until God started talking to me about the healing ministry I never thought about it. It never crossed my mind. I didn't even know there was such a thing as a healing ministry. But the word "healing" kept coming into my mind without my asking it to. Then people were sent to me who said the word "healing" again and again.

He doesn't force you to listen or to do something you don't want to do, but He does look for people who will do His work. If you are open to doing His work, He provides the strength and courage that you need. When you do the work He has asked you to do, it brings great satisfaction and fulfillment.

One way you can know if it's really God speaking to you is to pay attention to everything that goes on around you and listen to what's being said. God speaks to you in quiet moments, through dreams, through people, through books, through sermons — even through the mail!

So I wasn't overly surprised when one night I had a dream about the healing ministry. After all God had been talking to me about it for six years. And I was finally beginning to get comfortable with the idea that I actually could go into the healing ministry — whatever that meant.

I can't remember much of the dream. All I remember is hearing the words, "Healing ministry, do the healing ministry."

I woke up immediately and said, "Well, if you want me to do the healing ministry then send me someone to teach me."

Shortly after that a friend of mine told me I just had to — I must — go to a certain Christian conference. It was the Association of Christian Therapists International Conference in Alabama in 1999.

During the conference I was wearing a t-shirt that said the name of my church. I was walking into a workshop when a woman stopped me and said, "I go to that church, too."

It turned out she had just moved to East Central Florida and started attending that church. Now what are the chances of meeting someone at a conference more than 1000 miles from home that goes to the church in your hometown?

Coincidence? Maybe. God-incidence? Definitely. You wouldn't believe how much of a God-incidence.

So after chatting with her for about fifteen minutes I took my seat. I was sitting next to the same person who told me I had to go to the conference. He leaned over and asked me if I knew who I had been talking to. I said, "a lady that I met who goes to my church at home."

He said, "That's Barbara Shlemon Ryan. She's been in the healing ministry for 35 years."

When I heard that, my mouth dropped open.

Now, I know I asked God to send me someone, but you could have pushed me over with a feather just then.

Never Underestimate the Power of God.

Barbara Shlemon Ryan would soon become my teacher and mentor and I had gone nearly 1000 miles to find that she lived within five miles of me. That knocked my socks off. God had indeed sent someone to teach me about the healing ministry, only one month after I had asked for a teacher.

Barbara told me early on that if I wanted to get familiar with the healing ministry, I needed to go to the praise and worship prayer meetings at church. These prayer meetings included the laying on of hands, which I was already familiar with. It was at one of those prayer meetings that I first felt like God was saying the words "heal my people" to me.

I had told Barbara I was thinking about writing a book. I thought the book might help people heal emotionally as well as spiritually but hadn't a clue on how that was going to happen.

A journalist friend and I had talked for several years about doing this kind of book. She thought I had a story and a message that might help other people. But our schedules were always conflicting. The last time we had talked her schedule was full for nearly a year and it looked like a project that would happen — maybe — some day.

At the same time, as part of a growing need to share my faith I started meeting with Barbara and a fellow counselor in my office who is an Episcopalian (her name is Debbie, too.) Debbie and I had attended the Association of Christian Therapist's conference together. She brought her deacon,

Hazel, to our regular meetings. These weekly meetings, which still go on, consist mainly of prayer, sharing and talking about the needs of God's people. They also feed a beautiful friendship in Christ between four women of two different faiths.

During one of those early meetings with the other three women, I told them about hearing the words "heal my people." Both Barbara and the deacon, Hazel, turned around simultaneously, looked at each other and said in unison, "That's your book."

Two days later, the journalist faxed me a schedule of when she could work on the book, a book that now had a distinct theme and purpose. Coincidence? I don't think so.

That journalist, L. Frances Coker, helped write this book and she told me that she felt really pushed to find time to write and fax a schedule.

So I knew I was going to be writing this book but I still had to learn more about the healing ministry.

The funny thing is that all the time these meetings were going on and I was hearing the words "healing ministry" I was having trouble trusting that I was supposed to do this. I can't tell you how many books I purchased and read about healing to see if I could find myself in there. After hours and hours of paging through those books I still wasn't sure I was called to the healing ministry.

Healing Opportunity

However, God granted me an opportunity to find out that I was, indeed, called to the healing ministry.

I received a phone call from my brother on a Wednesday afternoon about two months after I started meeting for prayer with those three other women. The fact that he called me was quite unusual for him. I usually don't hear from him during working hours. He sounded really upset.

He told me he had received some bad news from his doctor. They had found a mass in his right lung. He's not a smoker but he has had terrible asthma all his life. The mass had been found during a routine yearly chest x-ray.

He was very scared. Understandably. I said, "No matter what, somehow we'll get through this." The doctor wanted him to have a magnetic resonance image (MRI) but couldn't schedule it for two weeks. On the same day he called, I had a meeting, that took me right past his office building. That was a bit of a God-incidence because normally I didn't go that way.

As I drove past his building, I kept feeling God wanted me to go lay my hands on him and pray.

I was very, very reluctant. My brother believes in God but has some reservations about things like laying on of hands. He's very intellectual and isn't comfortable with these kinds of things. By the time I had thought about all of this and was still feeling the need to do what I thought God wanted, I had driven by the building. Try as I might I just couldn't keep going; I had to turn the car around.

When I went in I was hoping he was busy and couldn't see me. But he wasn't. So in I marched and in the hallway I quietly told him, "If this had happened to a close friend of mine I would have laid hands on them and prayed. That's what I want to do with you."

To my surprise he said, "Right this way," and showed me to his office.

He called his secretary in to share in the prayer. The three of us prayed. I put my hand over his right lung and I asked God to heal him, to wipe away all traces of that mass and to restore his lungs with new healthy cells. I don't remember all the words because I cried all the way through the prayer. God knew that I wanted my brother healed. In a few minutes, the prayer was done. I gave my brother a hug and walked out of the office, still shaking from the whole experience.

I got back in the car, started talking to God and I cried some more. And I said, "Lord, if you really want me in the healing ministry it would be really great if my brother would be healed."

And I just surrendered it into His hands and let it go. I trusted that whatever happened would be what He wanted for my brother.

The day came for the MRI and then we waited another week for the results. And, guess what? They found nothing in his right lung. That mass was gone. Immediately after hearing the good news, I got on my knees and I cried as I thanked God. You see, he's my only sibling and I want him to stay around. So it was a great relief to hear he had been healed.

God is pretty hard to ignore, I thought. I took that healing as a sign that He really did want me in the healing ministry. I was finally convinced that I had to be obedient to God's call. I stopped reading all those books and began writing mine.

Mental Health and Spiritual Thoughts

In therapy, healing emotionally is also about obedience.

To get healthy emotionally you have to follow instructions and do things you may not have previously been inclined to do. You may not have been so inclined because the state of your mental health was blocking you. Healing emotionally also is about trusting and having faith that the person in front of you, the counselor or therapist, knows enough to get you to the other side of the pain. It all takes hard work and willingness — very hard work and lots of willingness.

And still there will be moments of doubt.

After all, we think, if the people in our lives would just change we wouldn't have to. But the truth is, it's all about us. We must be willing to work on ourselves and clear out our own stuff so we can move on in good spiritual and mental health.

Therapy sometimes doesn't feel good. I compare it to what it feels like after having surgery. Everyone has a recovery period when they need to just take it easy and nurture themselves through the process until they heal. It's the same with therapy. Counseling is like emotional surgery: you cut into the body of old stuff from the past — cut out the junk that continues to hurt you and lead you astray — and then sew up gently the wounds of the past. Then the real healing of wisdom, forgiveness and peace begins. If a client has spiritual beliefs, it's at this time that he or she opens to God's love and finds the path back to Him.

For those who don't have that belief I still work to link them to love in some way. For instance, I will suggest they spend time with a special loving, nurturing person in their life.

I tell all my clients to be good to themselves, forgive themselves and start to love themselves. I teach them how to nurture themselves.

To me, one of the best ways to nurture yourself is to talk to God. Beginning with that talk we had when I was under the altar, I have never stopped talking to Him. When I really need nurturing, I close my eyes and visualize myself as a child sitting at the feet of Jesus. He strokes my head and I feel His unconditional love and peace. Then I feel healed and ready to live in this world again.

Exercise

Sit back, close your eyes, relax and imagine yourself going to a special place of peace. It could be a garden or a quiet beach or next to a mountain stream, wherever you find peace. Now feel everything that's around you. Smell the smells of that special place. See all the beauty there just for you. Hear the peaceful sounds of your surroundings. Relax and just be there. Relax into the moment. Accept the peace and serenity that is yours for the asking. Breathe it in. Breathe deeply. Then exhale all that is worrying you. If you feel the need to have God there with you, ask him to come be with you.

Know you are special, special to God, and that you deserve to be loved. Feel that love. When you are ready and have gotten what you need, you can come back to the here and now, bringing that peace, serenity and love with you. Feel your feet on the floor and open your eyes to a new beginning.

Prayer

Dear God,

Thank you for Your unconditional love and mercy. We are a wounded people and You are the great healer. Help us to be open to coming to You. Help us to find You and immerse ourselves in Your Living Waters of healing. Help us to be cleansed in those waters and come out renewed and healed so that we might have new life and have it abundantly. We ask all of this in Your Son's name, Jesus. *Amen.*

Heavenly Father

Thank you for the great joy you have placed in my life, for the serenity, and the peace. Help me to live in the present where your peace and grace are always there for me. Help me to share my sense of peace with others so they, too, might experience your grace and love as I have experienced them. Heavenly Father, there are times when words fail and all I can express is awe for the difference you have made in my life. I thank you and praise you for that difference and I ask all that I ask in Jesus' name, *Amen*.

Love, L. Frances Coker
(Co-author)

Chapter 12

Peace Beyond Understanding

John 14:27 of the Bible states, "Peace I leave with you; my peace I give to you. I do not give to you as the world gives. Do not let your hearts be troubled, and do not let them be afraid."

"The Peace of God, which passeth all understanding keep your hearts and minds in the knowledge and love of God, and of his Son Jesus Christ our Lord: And the Blessing of God Almighty, the Father, the Son and the Holy Ghost (Spirit), be amongst you, and remain with you always. Amen." *Book of Common Prayer*, 1928.

Peace on a Platter

I was not born with peace on a platter. I grew into it the hard way. I used to whine about going to church when I was a child. I was a rebellious teenager and when my best friend was brutally murdered I was tortured with her pain and my loss for months on end.

My first sense of the peace which passes all understanding came after I crawled out from under the altar all those years ago, walked down the aisle and opened the church doors to leave. As I touched the doors I felt showered with relief and peace that I never had felt before. The heavy, almost physical, burden of grief and guilt was lifted then and there, never to return.

I sought to hold onto that feeling as long as I could and feed it. But it took a long time for me to figure out how to surrender to God. I had to grow and mature in faith.

The next time I felt that overwhelming peace beyond my understanding came after another hard experience. I had a miscarriage and was again in deep grief. Through the help of a compassionate friend I did a visualization of handing my baby over to Jesus. As I handed the baby over the same peace as before fell upon me.

I had several more such experiences but in between them I still didn't have true peace in my life until I learned to surrender moment by moment to God.

Challenge to Surrendering

One of the first challenges to surrendering came after my mother died and my father became very ill. Andy and I talked about having him move in with us because every other week I would drive two hours to check on him, stay for about three hours and drive the two hours back. It was grueling to say the least. Finally, we made the decision to have him move in with us and we built a handicapped-accessible room onto our house. He had already experienced both a stroke and a heart attack and was using a cane when he moved in. Within three years of moving in he had a second major stroke on the other side of his body and almost died.

He was sent to a rehabilitation facility and grew stronger for the first three weeks but then started to get sick again and took a turn for the worse. He asked us to bring him home so he could die in peace (which he did, not then, but several years later). However at that time, after three weeks of no sleep, heavy arguments, tension, anxiety, and children crying for lack of attention, we all were pretty exhausted. All my friends and family in my emotional support system were telling me it was time to put him in a nursing home. Before my mother died, however, she had made me promise never to do that. Of course, the battle was mine and nobody else's. I struggled and argued with everyone until one night I reached the end and found myself on my knees crying out to God. The next day the certified nursing assistant, who watched him while we were working, called an ambulance because he was so sick. And he was put back in the hospital. After two weeks the hospital transferred him to a nursing home and wouldn't let me take him home. It no longer was my decision. Surprisingly, it was the nursing home, which brought him back to life. Then he was able to be back home with us for the last six years of his life. To me the good outcome of this situation is directly attributable to surrender. And it was the surrender in prayer that night that brought me peace.

More Surrendering

Another such surrendering moment came when helping my daughter Krystle through some tumultuous early teen years. She seemed to struggle with mood swings and most of the time she was very down. Both my husband's family and my family have a history of depression running through them, so her depressed moods concerned me.

I started to search for help and I prayed. I prayed *over* her. I prayed *for* her. I put her on prayer lists and I kept on praying and searching. As a counselor I wanted to fix this problem by myself. Although I had given this situation to Him in prayer, I kept taking it back from God. I put her in counseling (for those who don't know — the ethics of counseling require that someone not related counsel family members) and then went the regular medical route for medication. Her condition left me stymied because nothing was helping. The more I tried to fix it, the worse it got. Finally, I realized I would have to let God help me find the answers, wherever they came from. So I used the Internet to search for people who might have experience in this area. I was given the name of a woman who had a teenager who was very depressed but who had been helped by Chinese herbal medicine. This *really* took surrender on my part. But God is good. That woman actually met me at the office of her Chinese herbal practitioner. Within three months he had healed Krystle when nobody else had been able to. It was a gift from God. The peace it brought into my life is phenomenal. I had felt like I had been on a roller coaster for three years and God had finally helped me get off — but first I had to entirely surrender the situation to Him.

Now, when I start to obsess about something or find myself stuck on things that cause me distress I know it's time to pray and surrender. After years of testing this, I can tell you from personal experience that prayer and surrender work. Again, the answer may not be what we expected but our prayers are heard. For me, so many prayers have been answered that I no longer need to be reminded to pray.

Willing to be Willing

Prayer comes as naturally as breathing. That doesn't mean some things aren't very hard to surrender. When I find I have trouble surrendering — that is giving a problem to God to fix instead of trying to fix it myself and thus making a muddle of it -- I simply ask for the grace "to be willing to be willing" and to let go.

When we pray it's because we are not at peace with ourselves or we need a situation to be taken care of in our lives or the lives of others. We are asking for a change so that we might have peace. We find peace by surrendering our needs to God. When we allow God to be in control, every part of our life just gets better and better.

Mental Health and Spiritual Thoughts

When my clients come to see me, they, like most people in life, are looking for happiness. They are searching for this elusive quality in the bottom of bottles, with food, with material things, with the help of pills and other drugs, by doing too much and never stopping. They are looking for it through affairs, unfulfilling marriages and demanding jobs and any other dysfunctional behavior that will pretend to feed the need. Those of you reading this book know who you are.

Life does not deliver happiness or peace on a platter 24 hours a day.

People confuse the highs they get through dysfunctional behavior for true happiness. They are looking for immediate gratification. They come to see me when they have run out of steam and still find themselves miserable. Nothing else has worked.

My clients always say a version of, "I can't continue to live this way." They keep doing the same things expecting different results and that's one definition of insanity. Most of them are ready for the insanity to stop by the time they get to my office. They are finished with the dysfunction yet they don't even know if I can help them. But they sure hope I can, because they've been living life in circles.

And they are so afraid. Afraid of everything. Fear, I tell them, is "false evidence appearing real" according to the 12-step groups. People spend enormous amounts of energy in worry and anxiety about something that has not happened or become a reality. Because of their fears they miss the real things that are right in front of their face. Instead, they always seem to be looking to the future for a place where things will magically be better. Life is short. I tell my clients not to miss what's real and right in front of them: take pleasure in a sunset, a blue sky, a new baby, a puppy — the simple things that feed your soul.

I tell my clients true happiness, in my opinion, comes from within. It is when you become comfortable with who you are and you accept the failures and shadows of who you are, when you have no secrets and, most importantly, can forgive yourself and others, that you can approach happiness. Then you can be free of the turmoil and craziness.

A lot of this dysfunction — looking for happiness in all the wrong places — comes from our very human need to be in control of our lives. And then we try to control others in order to make ourselves happy. Of course, this sort of control only leads to unhappiness for everyone involved.

For many people I know, and many of my clients, getting to happiness means surrendering our need for control to God. When we surrender our need for control we experience a sense of relief.

This releases us from the struggle to make everything work in our lives. The false happiness (those former crazy highs — and the lows that follow) is gone, but true contentment, which comes from a lasting and secure inner peace, takes its place.

Exercise

When you become aware of dysfunctional behavior, look at it, acknowledge it and invite Jesus into it.

Sit quietly in a meditative way and wait for what He says or does. Hopefully, you'll experience some insight into the red flags of your dysfunctional behavior, meaning just what is it that triggers you to compulsively do things that are bad for you. Those triggers are based on unfulfilled needs, like the need to have control, power, approval, security or affection. You have to look deeply within yourself. What needs were not met in your childhood that have left you with empty holes in your soul? Trying to fill those holes in unhealthy ways creates the dysfunction.

It's important to work on the triggers of childhood because they will continue into your adulthood, unless you take time to acknowledge those childhood wounds.

To do this, I have my clients use their non-dominant

writing hand to write a letter from the little-wounded-child-still- within them to their adult. Then I have them use the dominant writing hand to respond as a loving, nurturing parent to that child. I tell them, also, to spend time rocking in a rocking chair with a blanket wrapped around them to soothe some of those old wounds. Most importantly, I tell them not to judge the process, just do it. They have to do some re-parenting of that little, wounded child inside them and feel the feelings before they can let go of the triggers to their dysfunctional behavior.

To further let go of this dysfunctional behavior, imagine a stream of love pouring from heaven into those empty holes in your soul filling them up. We know truly that our Creator can fill those empty holes better than anything or anyone else. For He truly is our Savior who saves us from ourselves.

Love is the Answer

Happiness comes to those who open their hearts to the peace of Christ.

He came to love us and show us how to love.

If you take nothing else from this book take this: *love* is the answer.

It is the beginning, the middle and the end. The first commandment is all about loving God. The second is about loving each other.

And it starts with you.

Lord, make me an instrument of your peace
Where there is hatred... let me sow love,
Where there is injury ... pardon,
Where there is doubt ... faith,
Where there is despair ... hope,
Where there is darkness, light,
Where there is sadness ... joy.

O Divine Master, grant that I may not so much seek
To be consoled ... as to console,
To be understood ... as to understand,
To be loved ... as to love.

For
It is in giving ... that we receive,
It is in pardoning, that we are pardoned,
It is in dying that we are born to eternal life.

St. Francis of Assisi

About The Author
Deborah A. Kalinyak

Deborah Kalinyak, a licensed mental health counselor in Central Florida, is gaining national attention for focusing on the need for spiritual health in the mental health arena. She often gives talks on this subject as well as leading seminars and retreats.

Kalinyak holds a master's degree in mental health counseling and has been in private practice for nearly a decade. She is a member of the Association of Christian Therapists, an international association of Christian health care workers. She is one of the founding members of the ecumenical Sacred Way Ministries, whose mission is to "minister to the ministers," to pray for, and spiritually feed, those lay people and pastors who are on the front lines serving God and His people.

Kalinyak is married and the mother of two teenagers.

For more information about Kalinyak's speaking and seminar calendar or to order additional copies of *Hope for the Wounded Heart,* please contact Sacred Way Ministries at 321-733-2625 or Day to Day Enterprises at 407-359-9356.